READY, SET, COACH!

Build a Thriving Coaching Business Fast

KRISTIN A. SHERRY
JUDITH C. SPEAR

Black Rose Writing | Texas

The author grants the final approval for this literary material.

First printing

Although the authors and publisher have made every effort to ensure that the information in this book was correct at press time, the authors and publisher do not assume and hereby disclaim any liability to any party for any loss, damage, or disruption caused by errors or omissions, whether such errors or omissions result from negligence, accident, or any other cause.

ISBN: 978-1-68513-048-0
PUBLISHED BY BLACK ROSE WRITING
www.blackrosewriting.com

Printed in the United States of America
Suggested Retail Price (SRP) $24.95

Ready, Set, Coach! is printed in Palatino Linotype

*As a planet-friendly publisher, Black Rose Writing does its best to eliminate unnecessary waste to reduce paper usage and energy costs, while never compromising the reading experience. As a result, the final word count vs. page count may not meet common expectations.

Editing: MEB

Dedicated in Memory of Rhoda Johns
(nee Rhoda Ann Rhodes)

READY, SET, COACH!

Build a Thriving Coaching Business Fast

CONTENTS

GET THE MOST OUT OF THIS BOOK

Throughout this book you'll see these icons:

 The pen notes an activity. These activities are for self-discovery or to reinforce concepts presented. Do these exercises to better internalize and learn from what has been shared. There are a lot of activities so you can choose the ones most helpful for you to complete.

The lightbulb calls out additional ideas you can implement in your coaching or in your business.

INTRODUCTION

The guidance in *Ready, Set, Coach!* is useful for any and all coaches, consultants, and small (service-based) businesses. This book was created from 40+ years of coaching and consulting experience from mother/daughter co-authors Judi Spear (mother) and Kristin Sherry (daughter). The original purpose of this book was to provide a trusted resource YouMap® coaches could refer to as they build their coaching practices.

Judi and I, Kristin, got together and reviewed our collective years of experience to outline what we wished we knew about the ins and outs of starting a coaching business, running that business, and working with clients. We laid out the topics we believed were most essential to share with coaches and business owners. Those conversations led to the content included in *Ready, Set, Coach!*

You'll not only gain knowledge from our experience but from stories of coaches we trust who have a wide range of experience in interesting niches. A few of the stories are presented in "Chapter 1: Coach Stories," while others are found throughout the book.

Since you're reading this book, we assume you are a coach, consultant, or small business owner who wants to increase your growth and impact or you are interested in becoming a coach, consultant, or business owner. Let's set the expectations for what you will find in this resource. The book is organized into three mains sections: "Ready," "Set," and "Coach!"

Throughout various sections of the book we offer activities to internalize the information you learn and suggest ideas for action. This book contains a ton of information. **Pace yourself.** Give yourself room to work through the content to avoid becoming overwhelmed. Complete the exercises that seem most beneficial. You could also partner with someone to work through some of the exercises. Share and discuss your results to make it collaborative and insightful. This book is not intended to be a one and done read. Think of it as a resource chest you can dip into again and again, based on your current needs – "The Coach's Bible," so to speak.

Following is a high-level overview of what is covered in the three sections of the book.

Ready – Get ready to become a coach or launch a business

In the first section, "Ready," we cover the most important considerations as you launch a coaching business. Even if you have launched a business or work as a coach for someone else these chapters will help you confirm if you have a strong foundation. We will share some coach stories to give you a sense if coaching is right for you and then help you figure out who you are as a coach.

We will guide you to decide if coaching or consulting is

a better fit for your talents. Coaching and consulting differ, and we explain how and why those differences can affect your career satisfaction. We will walk you through a process to define clients you want to work with and clients you want to avoid. You will receive guidance about building your brand, coaching certifications, starting a business, and the financial considerations of starting and running a coaching business.

Set – Put key things in place to set yourself up for success

In the second section of the book, "Set," we offer guidance to help you set up your business for success. Topics include messaging and marketing, client contracts and proposals, deciding on your services and how to price them, selecting a niche, client lead generation and softer selling strategies to attract clients. We will cover how to balance generosity with making money and end with vital step-by-step guidance to get the right assistant for you and the support you need.

Coach! – Learn to navigate coaching better, from discovery calls through best practices and proven tools to help your clients

In the third and final section of the book, "Coach!," we cover key topics related to coaching and execution within your practice. Topics include ethical considerations in coaching, time management and prioritization, coaching process and best practices, why using assessments and tools in your coaching business is a great idea, highlights of our favorite assessments, coaching tools, and coaching questions.

We also address how to deliver group coaching, guidance about speaking engagements, what to consider before partnering with other coaches, leveraging your expertise to create passive income, and things to know about writing a book to showcase your expertise. We end with the top ten reasons coaching businesses fail so you can see how this book has prepared you to succeed.

Our goal is to help you feel equipped and confident in more areas of your practice and reduce your guess work. We focus most on the areas where coaches tend to struggle or that are the most critical to your practice.

Many coaches are helpers, nurturers, advocates, and people who look to make a difference in people's lives. Yet, most coaches are often not savvy at running a business. Failed coaching and consulting businesses are often not a problem with coaching skills but, rather, a lack of the skill needed to run a business. So, this book will include key elements to build and run a successful coaching practice. We also know that coaches are largely on their own when it comes to coaching, so we will additionally equip you with a toolkit of powerful techniques, tools, and tips for coaching.

One important note about how this book is structured. Since *Ready, Set, Coach!* is authored by two people, we indicate the primary author for each chapter under the chapter title. Whenever the co-author contributes information or a story to a chapter, the passage will be *italicized* and prefixed with the co-author's name to make clear who is addressing you.

Now, let's get *Ready*.

PART I: READY

—————— ☙ ——————

The late author and speaker, Jim Rohn, said, "Part of success is preparation on purpose." I'm certain most people starting a coaching or consulting business, or those considering this path, make an effort to prepare. However, when starting something new, people often don't know what they need to know. It's easy to become overwhelmed with so many demands for your attention, so many things to learn, and precious little time to learn it.

As stated in the introduction, *Ready*, seeks to equip you with a solid foundation *before* you begin to coach. If you've already started coaching, that's okay – it's never too late to make improvements and incorporate elements from this section to strengthen your foundation. In fact, the first section of the book will likely trigger a few lightbulb moments for areas to improve and increase satisfaction in your work.

Let's jump into coach stories to gain insight through the eyes of other coaches.

1

∽ ❧ ∽

COACH STORIES
Kristin

Whether you are already working with clients or you're yet to start down this path, we begin the journey with coach stories. Every coach, regardless of experience level, can learn from other coaches. Stories reinforce why this work matters. You might relate with some coaches and their stories more than others. You also might notice you are wired quite differently than other coaches. There isn't one coach mold you must fit into. People with different talents, values, skills, and personalities can be effective coaches for different kinds of people. An analytical coach might attract engineers, for example.

We include a summary of takeaways from each story. As you read the stories, do they motivate and inspire you? Think about why you want to be a coach as you read this chapter, and how the takeaways might apply to you.

These coaches also share questions you can use to help clients gain clarity or make important decisions. You'll hear inspiring stories that will help you decide if coaching is for you. Some of these coaches work in niches you might not have known existed. We want you to expand your thinking as you explore different kinds of coaching.

We will introduce you to Victoria Volk, whose expertise is in grief recovery, Kerri Twigg, creator of *The Career Stories Method* and author of the book by the same name. You will meet Diane Roesch who uses executive coaching techniques with children who have experienced emotional trauma, and Amoreena Murray whose coaching niche helps coal miners transition out of a shrinking industry. We interviewed Natasha Knight who helps women of color advance in their careers or find their next appropriate role. Finally, we'll share three core principles of coaching through Dave Pennington's experience finding his niche as a coach and consultant for pastors. We'll begin with Victoria.

VICTORIA

When we interviewed Victoria, who helps clients unleash their heart from suffering, we began by discussing how effective coaches ask good questions rather than tell people what to do. Here's what Victoria had to say, followed by the rest of her interview:

"I'm a huge proponent of helping guide people to their own answers. It's in the deeper questions we find answers. I like to challenge people in their beliefs about what they know about grief, or what they've been taught."

What questions do you like to ask clients?

"I will often ask, 'Are you already suffering? Has what

you've been doing for your grief helped you? You might as well be suffering and move your feet.'"

You've been there, haven't you? You understand your clients. You understand what it's like to grieve for 30 years.

"I try to create a bridge to what they see in their life today and what it could be. I use myself as an example. When we fall into the trap of S.T.E.R.B.S. (short-term, energy-releasing behaviors), which are behaviors that make us feel better for a time, like alcohol, food, gambling, relationships, sex, shopping, or any behavior we take part in that runs on auto-pilot, we're not being intentional. That creates more shame in our lives. That's where I found myself, and it progressed."

Are there other questions you like to ask clients?

"One of my favorite questions is, 'What are you trying to forget?' It's not mine, but it's a really good question."

What has been your most challenging client experience?

"I've not had a terrible client experience yet. I'm blessed in that way. Those who've chosen to work with me really trust me. People are resonating with hearing about grief in a way they've never heard about it before. When people hear new knowledge, something they've never heard, they pay attention."

You coach what you know, right? You combine having been there yourself with having done deep work to gain new insights.

"Yes, because you can't be certified by the Grief Recovery Institute without having gone through the process yourself. When I went to get certified, I got really sick out both ends. It was like a purge. I knew what was coming. Thirty plus years of my grief was about to come out. It changed me. In grief recovery we say you either implode or explode. You implode with disease and sickness or you explode with behaviors like anger that you project onto everyone else."

Why did you choose to become a coach?

"I had tried other things, personally, to help myself. I had a life coach, I bought Tony Robbins' program. I did all these things to try to understand why I felt so f---ed up, to be honest. I just felt really screwed up. I was kind of having a mid-life crisis. My youngest started kindergarten and I had closed a business at that time, so it was like losing two babies. My identity was so wrapped up in these external things and these people that I was raising, and I didn't know what I was going to do with my life.

"So I convinced my husband that I needed a dog. I replaced these losses with a dog. I did exactly what we talk about in grief recovery. I replaced the loss, which is a myth in grief. I needed something to pour my energy into, this grief that I had. I had to channel it somewhere. I thought I felt better, I started blogging and writing, but then I had another loss that opened a can of worms for me and I realized I wasn't okay. So, I asked myself, 'How can I get okay?' That's when I went on Google and found the Grief

Recovery Institute."

What's the difference between what you tried previously and what eventually helped you?

"It was action-based and time-based. I knew going into it I wasn't going to have to sit on someone's couch for 12 months. And the skeptic in me, they solved that problem, too, because it's evidence-based. Also, grief is unique to you; it honors that individuality and each person's story."

TAKEAWAYS FROM VICTORIA'S STORY

1. Coaches guide clients to find their own answers.
2. Coaches encourage clients to challenge their beliefs to help them move forward.
3. Coaches must be mindful of S.T.E.R.B.S. (short-term, energy-releasing behaviors). With over forty kinds of losses, clients are dealing with at least one, regardless of the purpose of coaching. Examples are job loss, loss of a family member, empty nest syndrome, and divorce.
4. Coaches connect to clients through stories. People are more likely to trust those who have walked in their shoes.
5. Coaches share insights and knowledge to draw the right clients.
6. Coaches employ a standard process but leave room to honor the individuality of each person.

KERRI

I met Kerri through the LinkedIn professional networking platform about five years ago when she graciously agreed to contribute the section titled "Your Resume Tells a Story" in my best-selling book, *YouMap*. Kerri is one of the most successful coaches I know. Her business success has afforded her the freedom to create an intentional lifestyle which includes choosing who she works with and practices like daily mediation, walking her dogs, exercising, and writing.

How were you able to become successful as a coach?

"So, there are two things. People were coming to me for advice even before I was a coach. At one point, I was a community programs manager, but people were coming to me for advice about how to find a job, how to deal with their partners, or if they were nervous about doing a presentation.

"In many different jobs, the joke was that I was the resident life coach. I naturally had the skill, and I was naturally helping people and I didn't even realize how much I enjoyed it.

"The second thing that helped was I had a coaching job at a corporate firm. I was a career transition consultant. To land that job, I just told stories about how I was a volunteer at the children's hospital with terminally ill children. I would give their mothers breaks. And the way that I held myself and interacted with their child, they were like, *I feel safe enough with this volunteer with no medical experience. I feel comfortable with this volunteer sitting with my child while I go for a coffee or have a shower.*

"I told those kinds of stories to land a coaching job. The way that I coached was so unique and creative that when I left that job, within 10 days of leaving, corporate clients would call to say, 'I know you left but are you still coaching?'

"There was already a demand. They remembered my style, and so when they realized I wasn't there any more, HR Managers would say, 'You'd be the perfect person to coach my husband.' So my business really started with HR husbands in bars and cafés giving them career advice. So I was working with all these men who were kind of 'anti-coach.' People who, except that someone knew me, would never work with a coach.

"I had a non-compete with the HR firm so I couldn't publicly sell for a year. I could deliver services, but I couldn't advertise. So, the first year on LinkedIn, I didn't sell anything. I just went, 'Here I am, here's a story, here's a tip.' It was give, give, give. The interest in working with me grew because I didn't seem like a coach and people would say, 'This is the person I want to work with.'

"I was lucky to have three years at an HR consulting firm because I had stories to tell of real people experiencing job loss that I would share. I also had personal stories I would share. One of my most popular LinkedIn posts was about going to a job interview, and they said I had to do a presentation, and I wasn't ready.

"All I could think of was a presentation I had done the day before which was how to check a child's head for lice. So I acted out the story. 'And you part the child's hair, and you speak in a calm tone, and you look for nits.'

"It was this fancy building, and she [the interviewer] kept a straight face. But I told that story, and you would think you shouldn't tell a story about when you weren't prepared, talking about lice, but that was the post that led to my rise on LinkedIn.

"Other HR people and those in high stakes jobs who had done something embarrassing started sharing their stories. They knew I was vulnerable and so they could trust me."

What is the most rewarding coaching experience you've had?

"I know that the people who benefit from my style are usually people who don't hire coaches, probably should see therapists and don't, and feel like they can talk to me.

"My most rewarding client used to be a video editor who was burned out and quit his job. He came to me because a friend had a positive experience. And he said he was looking around at the other people he had worked with in media and said, 'They're so far ahead of me. I feel like I've screwed up my whole life. I'm a loser. I don't know what to say, and I don't know what to do.'

"The first thing we did was figure out his story, his skills of being a natural helper, streamlining processes, seeing the big picture and then being able to narrow into the little stuff. He said, 'Wow, you see all this stuff in me? I don't know if I can process that. I don't know if I can accept that.'

"I said, 'That's okay. I'll believe in you until you're ready to believe in you. Just see if a little piece of accepting, hey maybe I'm not a loser, could live in you.' I gave him a couple of mindfulness exercises to anchor away from his self-doubt and just focus on what he can see.

"So he would go to this café and work for a while, then on his way back he'd stop at this bench and do the meditation I taught him, which was see out and look at what you can see. At the end of that meditation he'd say, 'Okay, Kerri says I'm awesome at this,' and he'd start to feel good about it. Over a period of weeks he said, 'I think I am these things that you say I am.'

"When he got to a place where I knew he believed it enough, I suggested he reach out to some people he hadn't spoken to in a while to ask if they had any information on a role I thought he'd be a good fit. He started to contact people he hadn't spoken to in five years, and all of them were so happy to hear from him. Everything they remembered about him were the things I had been telling him. He felt they just thought he was a loser.

"These conversations led to a person referring him for a job as a product manager. Now he gets to oversee the creative process of other creatives and is making $170,000 from home at [a Fortune 100 Best Company]."

What was your easiest coaching assignment?

"I think the easiest was a girl who came to me who lost her job and was too scared to tell her mom because her mother had a heart condition.

"After four weeks of working together on a regular basis, on her resume and building up her scripts, it was causing stress that she hadn't told her mom. I told her I didn't want her to come back until she had told her mom. Because I'm a mom. She's going to know [something's wrong], she's going to feel it.

"So, she called her mother, because she knew I wouldn't see her, and she said, 'Mom, I lost my job.' Her mom said, 'Okay. What are you thinking you'd like to do next?' And so she said, 'I'm thinking I want to be closer to you. I still want to be an assistant, but I'd love to find a job near you.' And her mom responded, 'That's funny. I just got off the phone with Sheila and her assistant quit. Let me call her.' She got an interview that afternoon and had a job the next day."

TAKEAWAYS FROM KERRI

1. Coaching is built on a powerful desire to help people. Do you get out of bed in the morning to help others?
2. Coaches need to be able to quickly build trust. A principal element of an effective coach is clients feel safe with you.
3. Coaches whose primary motive is to sell are less likely to draw clients.

4. Coaches can attract clients through stories and should be willing to be vulnerable. Until people see themselves in your stories, they won't be moved to care.

5. Coaches who are clear on their ideal clients are more likely to work with the right people.

6. Coaches should be viewed by a client as a source of wisdom, which is made up of experience, knowledge, and good judgment.

7. Coaches help clients reveal and remove barriers.

DIANE

Diane started her career as a small business lender at a government agency. Her work involved meeting with small business owners to structure loans often considered too risky for traditional lenders. Diane's interest wasn't so much in calculating their credit worthiness but, rather, hearing their stories and dreams.

"I loved the conversations as small business owners were starting out. It was really fulfilling to work with them, learn every facet of their business and watch them grow.

"The businesses they were building were all different, yet everyone had a vision and similar challenges. I enjoyed that the investments they were making were in themselves. We were building up people with hopes for something better in the future and a process to get there."

Judi: In hindsight, Diane sees her Gallup CliftonStrengths themes in play. The CliftonStrengths assessment reveals a person's top natural abilities. The full 34 strengths are listed in the Appendix. Diane's Connectedness *saw the clients' vision,* Arranger *helped them with steps,* Positivity *encouraged them. Her* Maximizer *wanted to see them become all they could be, and* Input *collected the information they needed.*

Years later, Diane realized those conversations were really coaching – helping them flesh out their dreams while putting realistic steps in place. Today, Diane coaches middle and senior managers, in both non-profits and for-profits as well as volunteering with Edge Foundation, a not-for-profit which brings coaching to high-risk youth. Interestingly, Edge has found that youth, as well as adults, respond well to executive coaching tools.

What is the Edge Foundation?

"Edge Foundation was started by a retired entrepreneur who had two children who were diagnosed with ADHD. He recognized that executive coaching helped him stay on track in his career. So, he got an executive coach for his children and it worked. And that's how the Foundation came to be."

How did you get involved with Edge?

"I had a personal reason to get involved. I have a son who struggled in school and the teachers were punishing him with detention every day, and that was getting him nowhere. I instinctively knew Edge could help.

"We provide training to adults who work closely with youth in school and in after school programs and train them to coach by 'dancing in the moment.' By following the needs of the child and going where they need to go versus telling them what to do, youth build agency, accountability and problem-solving skills. Oftentimes, the coach might assume the problem is X, but by going where the child needs to go, they discover the issue is Y."

Who does Edge help?

"Edge coaches work with students anywhere from sixth grade through high school for just 20 minutes a week, and they make tremendous progress; from failing grades and challenging behavior, to passing all their courses and a better ability to manage their life, sometimes in as little as three months.

"Research shows that children with ADHD struggle with executive function in much the same way as children who have had adverse childhood experiences (ACES), such as poverty and homelessness, to living in a violent or toxic environment."

What do you enjoy about being a coach?

"What I appreciate about coaching, whether it's youth or adults, is that it's forward looking and positive. The person being coached is with someone who really cares about them, listens, does not judge and takes them through a process where they learn to deal with their challenges and solve their own problems.

"The youth often live in challenging circumstances or

struggle with ADHD. Some of the adults I coach had those challenges as a child and now they can understand them better as they deal with them in a work environment. It's transformational.

"Coaching for me is exciting. I just love the people I meet. I care about them and want them to succeed. Caring to me is listening, caring is support with tools, and sometimes caring is telling them what they don't want to hear. Throughout the process, I'm building relationships."

What advice would you give other coaches?

"First, change your questions – *tell me about, what* and *how* are great beginnings rather than *why*, which can feel judgmental. Non-directive and open-ended questions invite curiosity.

"Leave your data at the door. This isn't about offering solutions, it's about listening, showing empathy, building a trusting relationship.

"Be open to possibilities – Dance in the moment.

"Let the person you're coaching – adult or student – lead the way. You follow.

"Focus on their agenda.

"Keep it simple.

"Finally, try these five steps of coaching:

1. *Conversation*: Explore what's going on.
2. *Focus*: Where do they want to focus?
3. *Steps*: Break them down into pieces.

4. *Ask:* Invite them to share potential challenges: What could get in the way?

5. *Accountability:* How will you let me know you're making progress?

"Know that this process may seem slow at first. But to go fast, you must first go slow. And it requires patience. This is where invoking curiosity is helpful. Be curious about what you, the coach, will learn in the course of this conversation."

TAKEAWAYS FROM DIANE

1. Coaches can help clients see how their strengths reveal themselves even in roles that aren't a great fit. These stories are relevant to share in other contexts.

2. Coaches often have more experience than they realize. Did you informally coach the people in your life? Capture those stories.

3. Coaches can demonstrate empathy by finding a connection to a client's story. How have you walked in their shoes? Diane had a child with challenges, which created empathy and understanding toward the families she serves.

4. Coaches must remain open and resist making assumptions to help reveal a client's challenges.

5. Coaches can be a client's biggest supporter.

AMOREENA

I first met Amoreena in 2020 when she was a participant in a YouMap® Coach certification class. I'll never forget how she introduced herself. Amoreena said, "I help men stop eating and drinking their feelings." She explained that many of her clients, mostly men, didn't feel comfortable sharing their insecurities or failures with their wives or other men. She was a safe place for clients to be open and honest.

Amoreena initially worked with coal miners, but soon expanded to work with engineers, doctors, and other professional men who had multiple areas of their lives that weren't working for them. I wish you could have been a fly on the wall for Amoreena's interview. Her passion for helping people live a strengths and values-aligned life is unmatched.

Why did you choose to become a coach?

"I became a YouMap® coach because the day I got my YouMap®, within five minutes of reading it, everything hit me like a brick. I knew instantly why I was ending up on a stage feeling broken and empty while everyone was clapping for me. I'm receiving car keys and diamonds. I'm in the top two and three of sales for four years.

"The last two of those years I would physically get sick. I didn't know at the time my values were being violated. I felt like a spoiled brat. Everyone was like, 'You have this great life.' Status isn't even one of my values. My top values are love and connection, and I felt lonely. As soon as I saw my YouMap®, I resigned as a Sales Director.

"I thought there was something wrong with me, but it wasn't me. That's why I became a coach. I don't want people to sit and suffer. Time is not infinite. We can't get time back. We can get money back, we can get other things back, but not time.

"And the thing is, if I hadn't spent the time in that company worrying about all of that stuff I could have been a mom by now. I could have put that energy somewhere else if I had my YouMap®. So, that's why I became a coach. The handcuffs were off, the lights were on, and I didn't feel alone anymore. This can save people's lives."

What are some questions you like to ask clients?

"I like to say to people, 'Tell me about your day and tell me about yourself.' This [gets] people to speak from their values and speak about their strengths."

TAKEAWAYS FROM AMOREENA

1. Clients speak their strengths and values. If you listen closely to the words people choose, you learn a lot about their priorities and what's important to them.
2. Clients often aren't as self-aware as you might think, or as they might think! It's hard to read the label when you're inside the jar.
3. Clients benefit from your outside perspective. You are able to objectively synthesize what you hear. Never

underestimate the value and importance of this benefit of coaching.

4. Clients can appear to "have it all" on paper, yet experience guilt for feeling discontent. When our successes are not aligned to what's important (values), accomplishments feel empty.

5. Clients who are struggling are often "planted in the wrong soil." A fern can't survive, let alone thrive, in a desert. This is a powerful insight to share with clients.

NATASHA

Natasha works with women of color who are in a space where they're getting ready to make some sort of career decision. They either need to apply for a job because their position is ending, they're miserable in their job and simply need relief, or they want to find a better fit.

Who are the kinds of clients you most enjoy working with?

"I want to help women make transitions, to level up, whatever that looks like for them. I've got a client right now who is a lawyer and wants to become a yoga and wellness coach. Those are exactly the kinds of people I want to coach. I want to help women, especially women of color, who are trying to make these transitions after they've gotten whatever degree and realize they're still not happy and need to make a shift.

"Even when looking at women who are making moves for promotions. You still have to talk about yourself, but it's a whole new interview for some people. It requires you to articulate what your strengths are, why the position is important to you in the first place, how it aligns with your values and the skill set you want to use."

What are challenges you and other women of color face that make working with someone like you so important?

"For a lot of women of color, we're raised in households where you're supposed to be humble. You're not supposed to talk about yourself, you're not supposed to make a big deal about what you bring to the table because you don't want to seem arrogant or full of pride – whatever the cultural and sometimes spiritual perspective is.

"I think for a lot of us that means we don't ever learn to talk about ourselves in a way that demonstrates our value or allows us to fight for our worth in terms of salary and the position and type of influence we can have in a workplace. Because of that, when I say to a client, 'Do you know what your strengths are?' they say they know but don't know how to talk about it. Even when they get their report they're still like, 'This is great and this sounds like me, but I still don't know how to talk about me. I see it, but how do I talk about it?'

"The main thing is to learn how to talk about yourself and do so in a way that demonstrates confidence and is compelling so that other people say, 'She's right, that's exactly what I see her doing' or 'That's perfect for what we need in our company right now so let's hire her, or give her the promotion.'"

What are your favorite questions to ask clients to get them thinking or get over barriers?

"I'm always asking the basics like, 'Where are you now and where do you want to be? If you could have it tomorrow, what would your world look like? If someone handed you the key and you could open it, what would that look like for you?' The other question becomes, 'What do you need?' One of the questions I love from *The Coaching Habit* is, 'If you're saying yes to this dream, what are the other things you're saying no to?'

"I like to ask these questions because it helps me to understand what to draw out for them when talking about their strengths and especially when they're talking about their values. If we're trying to figure out how to get from A to B, your values are going to be hugely important in that. You don't want to be doing something that requires you to be heavily collaborative with people if you are all about autonomy and freedom.

"When talking about strengths, if people say they really don't know them I ask another basic question, 'What do other people tell you about yourself?' We're our own biggest critic so we assume other people are criticizing us when they often aren't. They realize people aren't just saying things to be nice. This is actually how they're showing up in the workplace or in whatever setting they're in.

"Understanding where [they] want to go helps me draw attention to their values and strengths so there's alignment. It gives people encouragement, motivation, and boosts their confidence."

What's your favorite story where you helped someone see their strengths and the result lit you up?

"When I first started coaching, I was working with someone in my network. When we started working on her strengths, she really studied them. She took her strengths report, the notes from our conversation, and her own notes and thought about how those strengths show up.

"She had an interview before our next session to talk about her values, and that studying she did landed [her] her dream job. She was able to talk about her strengths in such a way that they were able to say, 'We want you. Here's the job.' And she was someone who came in saying, 'I know what my strengths are. I don't know how to talk about them.' In just one session she latched onto her strengths and then had some language around it and could think how it shows up. She took it and ran with it, and she got what she wanted."

How did that client success impact you?

"It's a huge motivator to keep going as a coach. I don't take full responsibility, of course, it was coaching her through the process. It really is self-discovery, learning about themselves, as opposed to me saying, 'This is who you are. This is what you do.' It was hugely fulfilling and gratifying to be able to help her."

What is it about your values that make coaching matter to you?

"One of my top values is making a difference. If I can make a difference in someone else's life and help them to make the impact they want to make and the career progress they want to see. That, to me, is golden.

"It also strengthens my connections with other people. Another one of my top values is being able to have connections and a sense of belonging. If you're connecting with me, you belong. I want to belong to a group of women who are successful in their careers and who also are willing to help others do the same. It's not just about us. It's about what can we do to help someone behind us, or even who is walking alongside us who needs a little push or some encouragement.

"It's important for me to affirm others, and that's exactly what coaching allows me to do, and to empower them and to let them know they are seen. I think for women of color a lot of times in the workplace we feel like we're not seen. We're putting in a lot of blood, sweat and tears to move forward in our careers and sometimes we're just constantly overlooked for opportunities.

"But when you're working with a coach and they say, 'This is how I see you, this is how you're actually showing up. You belong here. And here's how I can help to affirm and empower you to make sure that others know that and move your needle forward a little bit.' Coaching speaks to a lot of my values."

What made you decide to start coaching?

"I decided to start coaching because I realized I was coaching others in a very informal way – a lot. I don't know that I would have called it coaching at the time. Students would reach out to me for mentorship, and it was really a combination of mentoring, consulting, and coaching.

"I thought if I'm going to do this I need to figure out a way to not always give so much time away for free. I still can't remember how I learned about YouMap®. I know I saw it on LinkedIn and I was intrigued with it. If I was going to get certified, that was where I was going to start. Because of having the YouMap® certification, I had the confidence to call myself a coach.

"I wanted to continue to help people but also knew I could not continue to give away so much time without adding some monetary value to it."

TAKEAWAYS FROM NATASHA

1. Coaching questions are simple but rarely asked.
2. Coaching people with shared experiences helps you understand their barriers.
3. Coaches can deliver tremendous impact. One session has the potential to transform. That's worth more than coaches give themselves credit for.
4. Coaches guide, clients do the work and own results.
5. Coaches should connect their values to their coaching.

ACTIVITY:

Reflect on the questions Judi and I asked the coaches.

Answer some of the questions, yourself.

What are some of your takeaways from the stories?

How will you use them going forward?

The 3 C's of Coaching

Judi: The 3 C's of Coaching are core principles that are important to remember. What you learn in this book will help you honor these principles. Kristin will explain each one, and why it's important. The next chapter has exercises to apply the 3 C's of Coaching to yourself.

1. *Coach what you know.*
2. *Combine what you know with your abilities.*
3. *Care deeply about the work.*

Coach What You Know

You might be tempted to offer services or seek clients where you believe, or have been told, the biggest financial benefit exists. For example, coaches are often (wrongly) advised to seek corporate clients because of the higher rates they often deliver compared to coaching private individuals. But, if you're burned out from working in a corporate environment, that might bring you stress rather than joy. If you've never worked in a corporate setting, you could struggle to gain entry and/or credibility. Make sure money is not the primary reason you choose your path.

Others are often advised to pursue group coaching over individual coaching to obtain higher dollar workshop fees. What if you're someone who derives the most satisfaction from building deeper one-on-one relationships? While group coaching can be effective and satisfying for many coaches, others might feel something is missing when working in a group setting.

Dave is a coach and a consultant who once thought he should pursue corporate clients to financially maximize his coaching practice. Now he is a church consultant and pastoral leadership coach. With thirty years of ministry and non-profit experience, Dave understands the struggles of leadership in ministry and not-for-profit settings.

He has personally experienced the joys and struggles of leading a local church ministry. Dave is intimately familiar with the requirement of wearing multiple hats and leading at a high level over multiple functional areas in a ministry environment.

Dave also understands it's only a matter of time before a ministry leader's weaknesses begin to surface. He helps pastors raise their leadership ceiling and move from stressed to strategic pastoral leadership so they can joyfully serve God and others without having to work 50-80 hours every week or neglect their own family.

Pastoral leadership is stressful and, as a coach, Dave is well suited for this niche because he comes from that world of work. Prior to ministry consulting, however, Dave began to pursue coaching leaders in the for-profit world but soon concluded this decision wasn't in the best interest of his business because he lacked corporate leadership experience.

Could Dave competently coach leaders in a corporate context? Absolutely. Dave is smart, strategic, and understands leadership challenges. Would leaders in a corporate setting respond to Dave's sales attempts with skepticism given his lack of corporate leadership experience? Absolutely.

You will have a chance to reflect on coaching what you know in the exercises in "Chapter 2: You, the Coach." Let's review the second principle.

COMBINE WHAT YOU KNOW WITH YOUR ABILITIES

Not only does Dave coach the right clients in the right settings based on what he knows, he also knows *why* he excels. His top strength, according to the CliftonStrengths assessment, is *Strategic* thinking. Dave is a natural at helping pastoral and non-profit leaders grow and increase their organization's impact in their communities through strategic planning.

Another of Dave's CliftonStrength themes is *Maximizer*, the ability to help move people into roles where their greatest potential can be lived out. Maximizers are geniuses at taking people from good to great. The *Maximizer* theme equips Dave to help pastors gain clarity about themselves so they can properly align their ministry roles and responsibilities with how they're wired and build a complementary team so the ministry can reach its goals. Dave is a perfect example of *marrying what you know with your natural abilities*.

People won't hire you for your degrees, they will hire you for your experience. Everyone has experience somewhere. Where is your experience? You might be wondering how to figure out the intersection between what you know and your natural abilities. We have you covered in the next chapter. Let's look at the third principle.

CARE DEEPLY ABOUT THE WORK

Coaching is demanding. Without deep interest or passion, you won't stick with it. When I left the corporate world to strike out on my own, I focused on executive coaching because, like Dave, coaches and consultants told me that's where I would make the most money. Even though I'm not primarily motivated by money, I felt a self-imposed pressure to bring in revenue to prove I didn't make a mistake quitting my job. Also, fewer clients at a higher fee meant I wouldn't have to hustle for as many clients. That sounds great, right?

In theory, it seemed like a solid plan. Sales is draining for me, so the less I had to engage in sales activities, the better. However, there was a problem. I didn't have a great deal of passion for executive coaching. Judi, on the other hand, *loves* executive coaching. Even though I helped clients break through challenges or helped them gain valuable insight to apply to their situation, there wasn't fire in my belly for this kind of coaching. If you don't have passion or deep interest in your work, you will struggle to sell your services and risk not being highly engaged, which is unfair to clients.

Judi: As mentioned previously, I absolutely love executive coaching! I began my career 40 years ago as an administrative assistant and, even back then, executives sought me out to discuss a range of issues. I never knew why until 20 years later when I learned I was a strategic thinker. Instinctively, I knew the right questions to ask.

That ability has helped me across a wide range of situations. Executive coaching gives me significant impact because the people I coach have a span of influence over hundreds of people. When I impact them, they impact others. I've spent decades in the corporate world, so I feel right at home there and am familiar with all the relevant issues.

THE ROLE OF A COACH

Judi: One of my philosophies is that the role of a coach is to encourage a person about his or her situation and move that person to action. Coaches should be clear about how they encourage others and how they move people to action. In "Chapter 2: You, the Coach," Kristin will walk you through an exercise to do this.

The job of a coach is to encourage people about their situation and move them to action.

When someone speaks with you on a call, or connects with you at an event, if he doesn't feel encouraged about his situation after speaking with you, he isn't going to work with you. Keep these questions in mind:

How can I encourage this person?

How can I move this person to action?

How you encourage a client depends on your unique talents. For example, clients can be encouraged through wisdom, empathy, ideas, stories, casting an inspiring vision of the future, and many other ways. When you dig into your treasure chest of talents, you will discover what tools you have available to encourage clients.

Additionally, if your coaching doesn't move a person to action, you will not live up to your client's expectations.

Inspiration without action is just an expensive pep talk. As my colleague Nola always says, *the magic is in the action.*

How you move people to action also depends on your talents. Do you help people act through creation of easy-to-follow plans, generating a sense of urgency, persuasion, accountability, threats? (Kidding!)

We've introduced you to the basic framework of coaching. More in depth information with be found in "Part III: Coach!" After reviewing the coach stories and the basics of coaching shared in this chapter, you should have a sense if coaching feels right for you.

Next, I'll help you reflect on how you encourage people and move them to action in the next chapter. There are several self-discovery exercises you will need to do to build the necessary foundation. So, let's get started.

2

⁓ CƷ ⁓

YOU, THE COACH
Kristin

This chapter is a roadmap to find your way to yourself. The purpose of *You, the Coach*, is to provide frameworks, exercises, and insights for you to deepen your understanding of *you*. I train coaches in my work, and you might think coaches know themselves better than anyone. As the saying goes, "The shoemaker's children go barefoot."

Quite often, however, coaches are either unable to pinpoint what makes them unique as a coach, or they don't have the language to explain their impact succinctly and clearly. I recently met with Danielle who jokingly shared that it takes a half hour to explain what she does and how she helps clients. You should be able to do this in 20-30 seconds. When you know what you do best that other people need most, this becomes much easier.

Investing intentional time to develop a clear understanding of who you are has abundant practical uses. In upcoming chapters, I will guide you to build upon the insights you gain in this chapter for a variety of applications, such as:

- Deciding if you prefer coaching, consulting, or both
- Profiling your ideal clients
- Crafting a stand out brand and clear messaging
- Choosing service offerings that energize you
- Finding, or narrowing, your niche
- Using powerful, branded language to attract clients
- Pinpointing your gaps to hire the right assistant

Most advice for coaches employs a cookie cutter approach. Countless processes and programs exist promising coaches six or seven figure businesses. One concern with these programs is they offer strategies which were effective specifically for the *creator* of the program.

Often, coaching programs aren't proven to be repeatable for those who are wired differently than the individual who experienced success, assuming he has been successful. Unfortunately, marketers have been known to craft online personas which might not reflect reality. Beware of sales people who offer little more than a slick brand to attract eager-to-succeed coaches. Any successful program must, at minimum, offer repeatable results in spite of individual differences.

For example, I've seen posts on social media trying to convince coaches and business owners that, "You must create video to succeed in today's competitive market!" And they follow that statement with a sales pitch to their video course. Most "you must be doing x-y-z to succeed" advice is nonsense. The only thing you *must* do is play to your strengths and avoid trying to be something, or someone, you're not. As an example, you might come across slightly wooden on video but write extremely persuasively. In this example, blogging in your area of expertise would be a better strategy over video creation. If you like to write, you will attract clients who prefer to read content rather than watch it. Doesn't that make more sense? Individual differences matter.

Ready, Set, Coach! keeps you, the individual, in mind throughout the book. Advice can be brittle because it doesn't take context into account. This is especially true for coaching advice more than, say, accounting advice. I guide you using exercises and approaches that yield personalized results for you rather than issuing blanket advice. Often, this will be done through effective questions. Where advice constricts, questions open and create.

Where advice constricts, questions open and create.

You were advised in the introduction that this book contains a lot of information and exercises. *Again, pace yourself.* Growth and discovery is a process that takes time. To capture and get the most from your self-discovery data, I created the *Coach Canvas* which can be found in the *Appendix* of the book to make it easier to access and update as you complete certain exercises. Not all activity data is placed in the *Coach Canvas*. You will be instructed to enter your results in the *Coach Canvas* for the relevant exercises.

THE COACH CANVAS

The *Coach Canvas* gives you a snapshot of your data. The following illustrates a final product. Once your canvas is complete, I'll show you how to use it. The top section: *Strengths, Top Values, Top 5 Skills, Interests,* and *Traits* are covered first.

SAMPLE COACH CANVAS

Strengths	Top Values	Top 5 Skills	Traits
Maximizer	Love/Connection	Innovate	Encouraging
Futuristic	Faith	Strategize	Enthusiastic
Strategic	Autonomy	Write	Insightful
Ideation	Making a	Ideate	Resourceful
Input	Difference	Instruct/Train	Strategic
	Fun		Curious
	Balance	**Interests**	Imaginative
	Creativity	Thinker	Creative
	Meaningful Work	Persuader	
	Wisdom		
	Achievement		

How I Encourage Clients	How I Move Them to Action
I recognize and pinpoint greatness in people and help them see it, clearly and convincingly.	I generate strategic ideas clients have not considered, along with practical steps to take.

My Background/Experience	My Unique Contribution
Industries: Healthcare, Education, Training, Coaching Roles: Operations Management L & D Leadership	Strategic and visionary leader who maximizes others to achieve greater success through the creation of innovative programs.

Ideal Client Traits	Who I Help
Self-motivated Avoids excuses Achievement-oriented Service-oriented	Coaches, Leaders, Consultants, Career Counselors, HR Professionals

Let's begin exploration with *The Four Pillars of Career Fit*™

THE FOUR PILLARS OF CAREER FIT™

The Four Pillars of Career Fit™ is the heart of the YouMap® coaching framework.

In my research and work, I discovered that career fit and satisfaction boils down to four core factors. The following graphic visually outlines *The Four Pillars of Career Fit*™. I will expand on each pillar, explain how the pillars interact, then connect each of the pillars to actual coach stories.

THE FOUR PILLARS OF CAREER FIT™

HOW YOU WORK (STRENGTHS)	WHY YOU WORK (VALUES)
WHO YOU ARE (PERSONALITY)	WHAT YOU ENJOY DOING (SKILLS)

PILLAR ONE: HOW YOU WORK
(STRENGTHS)

How you work reveals your *priorities*. Your priorities are determined by your talents or natural *strengths*. Our strengths fall into one or more of the following four categories:

Relationship-building – people who relate one-on-one with others through natural abilities such as having empathy, being an encourager, a natural coach, teacher, mentor, or displaying ease in making connections with anyone. *Relationship-builders like to build deeper, meaningful one-on-one connections and prioritize working with people.*

The *Relationship-building* CliftonStrengths are *Adaptability, Connectedness, Developer, Empathy, Harmony, Includer, Individualization, Positivity,* and *Relator.*

Influencing – people who move others to action through natural abilities such as persuasive communication, confidence in one's decisions, inspiring others, boldness, or an ability to draw others out. *Influencers like to work with a variety of new people and prioritize working through people.*

The *Influencing* CliftonStrengths are *Activator, Command, Communication, Competition, Maximizer, Significance, Self-Assurance,* and *WOO* (Winning Others Over).

Executing – people who focus on tasks and employ natural talents such as achievement, accountability, discipline, consistency, efficiency, and focus. *Executers prioritize getting results.*

The *Executing* CliftonStrengths are *Achiever, Arranger, Belief, Consistency, Deliberative, Discipline, Focus, Responsibility,* and *Restorative.*

Thinking – people who process the world through thinking such as generating ideas, learning, envisioning, strategy, analysis, and curiosity. *Thinkers prioritize mental activity.*

The *Thinking* CliftonStrengths are *Analytical, Context, Futuristic, Ideation, Input, Intellection, Learner,* and *Strategic.*

Some people have a strength in each of the four categories, while others might have all five of their top strengths in a single category. It's also possible to have strengths represented in two or three categories. There is no right or wrong distribution. If you have strengths in one category, you are a strengths "specialist" which means you concentrate most of your time in one category, such as *thinking.* If you have strengths in each of the four categories, you are a strengths "generalist" and can shift between them!

Which strength categories do you identify as your priority? *Relationship-building? Influencing? Executing* (getting results)? *Thinking?*

Enter your strengths in the *Coach Canvas* in the "Strengths" section of the canvas found in the *Appendix*. You can add your top five CliftonStrengths, if you know them, or add the strengths categories most like you, such as *relationship-building* and *executing* or *relationship-building, influencing*, and *thinking*. Feel free to modify the words to suit you: *persuader* instead of *influencer*, or *result-driven* instead of *executer*.

PILLAR TWO: WHY YOU WORK
(VALUES)

"Why" you work reveals what's most important to you – your *values*. When values are honored, life feels more purposeful. When values are violated, life feels more stressful. At work, values can be honored or violated at three levels: the role, the manager, or the organization/environment.

For example, if you value collaboration, this value can be violated by the role if the job is isolated and not collaborative by nature, such as data entry. At the manager level, collaboration can be violated through a management style that inhibits collaboration. At the organizational level, the organization or culture might not promote collaboration.

Knowing your values is important because it aids decision-making and helps you set and defend boundaries. Our values are non-negotiable. It is unsustainable to live with violated values. The more violations, the greater the toll on your well-being.

 ACTIVITY:

Discover your values.

Review the list of values below and consider times in your life when you felt happy, proud, and fulfilled. When your values are honored, you will experience these emotions more frequently.

Select up to 10 values from the list.

Achievement	Contribution	Inner Harmony	Security
Adventure	Creativity	Kindness	Service
Authenticity	Curiosity	Knowledge	Spirituality
Authority	Determination	Leadership	Stability
Autonomy	Fairness	Love/Connection	Status
Balance	Faith	Loyalty	Success
Beauty	Freedom	Making a Difference	Trust
Boldness	Fun	Meaningful Work	Wisdom
Challenge	Generosity	Pleasure	
Community	Growth	Recognition	
Compassion	Happiness	Respect	
Competency	Honesty	Responsibility	

Next, prioritize your values by completing the exercise below.

Look at the first two values and ask, "If I could satisfy only one of these values, which would I choose?" For example, "If I could have all the *accomplishment* I wanted, but no *freedom*, or all the *freedom* I wanted, but no *accomplishment*, which would I choose?"

Ask this question until your values are ordered most to least important, with the most important at the top.

MY TOP VALUES

_____

_____

_____

_____

_____

_____

_____

_____

Idea for Action Enter up to 10 values into the *Coach Canvas* in the "Top Values" section of the canvas found in the *Appendix*. Your values are important as you think about services you offer, the kinds of clients you work with, and how you structure your business.

PILLAR THREE: WHAT YOU ENJOY DOING (SKILLS)

Skills are where the rubber meets the road. What do you enjoy spending your day doing? What does your ideal day look like? The answer to these questions reveals your *preferred skills*.

Strengths and skills are different. Strengths are natural abilities you're born with and skills are learned through experience.

Do you enjoy skills that relate to administration, supervision, leadership, sales, research and analysis, conceptual or creative, interpersonal, managing processes or projects, or technical and mechanical?

How we spend time contributes to feeling energized, neutral, or drained by our work. Spending more than 20 percent of the day on least preferred skills leads to burn out. When we don't spend enough time using preferred skills, we feel bored or under-utilized. Keep this in mind as a business owner. You have control over how you spend your day. The skills assessment is an eye-opening visual to help you make changes so work feels energizing, not draining.

Add 5-10 skills you do *best* and *enjoy most* into the *Coach Canvas* in the "Top 5 Skills" section of the canvas found in the *Appendix*. Your skills are important as you think about services you offer and what support you need from contractors, employees, and an assistant.

PILLAR 4: WHO YOU ARE
(PERSONALITY)

Who you are refers to *personality*. I will cover two aspects of personality: *interests* and *traits*. **Our personality shapes both our interests and our traits.** The personality pillar of *The Four Pillars of Career Fit*™ is based on interests, but I will also cover traits. Our traits refer to characteristics such as being *enthusiastic, bold, dominant, quiet, cautious,* and *supportive.*

I most often use the terms "traits," or "personality traits" and "interests," or "personality-based interests," rather than "personality." I will first discuss *interests,* then *traits.*

Personality-Based Interests

Our personality-based *interests* tell us a lot about our preferences. A research study of the Holland RIASEC, also known as the *Six Vocational Personality Types*, showed that the interests of teenagers, measured by the Holland types, were stronger predictors of employment and income than general personality assessments 10 years after leaving high school.[1]

In other words, *interests more strongly predict employment choices than general personality assessments that do not reveal interests.* The six Holland interest types are *Realistic, Investigative, Artistic, Social, Enterprising,* and *Conventional.* I refer to nicknames for the six types to make them easier to remember. They are the *doer, thinker, creator, helper, persuader,* and *organizer.* Everyone's interests are based on a blend of these types and one's interests align to the strongest two. Maybe you like to organize and create? Think and persuade? Do and help?

The Doer:

Doers prefer work that involves practical, hands-on solutions to problems. They value things they can see, touch, and use. They like to work with their hands, often work outside with machinery, tools, or animals. Unless they are coaches in sports or other physical endeavors, most coaches are not principally doers.

The Thinker:

Thinkers are intellectual, curious, and reserved. They like to solve problems and engage in challenges. They often choose work that involves ideas and heavy mental lifting.

The Creator:

Creators are imaginative, creative, original, independent, and expressive. They are inspired to create through activities such as music, writing, drawing, dance, photography, or art.

The Helper:

Helpers are interested in serving society and making a difference. They like to help people, and their work is most often centered around others. They are helpful, friendly, loyal, generous, and trustworthy. They gravitate toward nonprofit, education, healthcare, and social work.

The Persuader:

Persuaders often deal with business, leadership, or politics. They are involved in making decisions, starting up and carrying out projects. They like selling ideas or things and are generally energetic, ambitious, dominant, outgoing, and competitive.

The Organizer:

Organizers provide the structure, process, and order that organizations need to run effectively. They are generally methodical, detail-oriented, cautious, organized, responsible, and quality-oriented. Organizers are the glue that hold an organization together.

What Are Your Top Two Interest Types?
Read the descriptions and choose the two most like you.

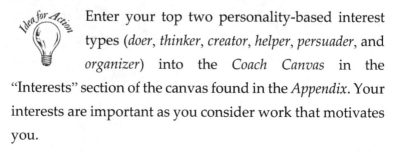 Enter your top two personality-based interest types (*doer, thinker, creator, helper, persuader,* and *organizer*) into the *Coach Canvas* in the "Interests" section of the canvas found in the *Appendix.* Your interests are important as you consider work that motivates you.

Once you've reached this point in the exercises, your *Four Pillars of Career Fit*™ are complete. I have a few more exercises coming in this chapter to enable you to complete most of your *Coach Canvas.* One remaining box on your *Coach Canvas,* "Ideal Client Traits," will be covered in "Chapter 4: Your Ideal Clients."

Take a break if you have exercise-burnout. Come back to the exercises when you're ready. If you're ready to continue, let's carry on!

PERSONALITY TRAITS

We all have positive personality traits, but often don't take time to name them.

A few years ago, I worked with a client who mentioned she hired me because she was drawn to my practical approach. She searched for coaches in her area, and I came up in the results along with another gentleman. She mentioned she didn't hire him because he used too many exclamation points on his website.

My client immigrated from the Netherlands where, she explained, people are friendly yet direct and realistic. The other coach didn't feel like a fit with her personality traits. On the flip side, a different prospective client might be uninspired by a practical approach and desire to work with someone with a bit more flair.

You don't need to act more gregarious than you are or act more reserved than you are because someone told you or implied that you should. Your personality traits are a big factor in who is drawn to you. Don't be afraid to show exactly who you are.

ACTIVITY:

Following is a list of personality traits. This activity is an easy way to identify your best characteristics.

Reflect on your temperament, character and outlook on life.

Highlight words that best describe you. Be as honest and objective as possible.

Ask people who know you to select words to describe your best qualities for more feedback.

Accountable	Dependable	Inclusive	Productive
Activating	Determined	Independent	Professional
Adventurous	Disciplined	Insightful	Rational
Affectionate	Distinctive	Intelligent	Realistic
Ambitious	Dynamic	Intuitive	Reassuring
Analytical	Efficient	Kind	Receptive
Articulate	Empathetic	Knowledgeable	Resourceful
Assertive	Encouraging	Likeable	Responsive
Attractive	Energetic	Logical	Self-aware
Bold	Enterprising	Negotiator	Sensitive
Bridge Builder	Entertaining	Objective	Sincere
Caring	Enthusiastic	Open-minded	Sociable
Charismatic	Ethical	Optimistic	Spontaneous
Charming	Expressive	Orderly	Steady
Cheerful	Fair-minded	Organized	Stimulating
Committed	Fast-paced	Original	Storyteller
Compassionate	Flexible	Outgoing	Strategic
Competitive	Focused	Patient	Strong
Confident	Friendly	Perceptive	Thoughtful
Congenial	Gentle	Persistent	Trusting
Connector	Genuine	Persistent	Truthful
Conscientious	Graceful	Persuasive	Unconventional
Cooperative	Happy	Planner	Unpretentious
Creative	Helpful	Poised	Vigorous
Curious	Humorous	Practical	Visionary
Decisive	Ideates	Precise	Warm
Dedicated	Imaginative	Problem Solver	Wise

Add 5-10 of your selected traits into your *Coach Canvas* in the "Traits" section. Choose traits people admire or value most about you based on feedback you've been given.

ACTIVITY:

Write a story about your traits benefitting someone, using 1-3 traits. A person who is *creative, analytical,* and *resourceful* has a different approach to coaching than someone who is *inclusive, empathetic,* and *encouraging.*

Here is an example to help with the activity:

Rhonda's traits are *strategic, wise, empathetic,* and *ideates.* She has an ability to pinpoint what keeps a person stuck.

Her *empathetic* trait causes her to listen and hear unvoiced concerns. Her *strategic* trait helps her zero in on the true problem. Her *wise* trait offers profound insights. Her *ideates* trait helps her offer ideas to solve problems.

_____

_____

_____

_____

_____

_____

How do your personality traits help your clients?

 Emphasize your best traits everywhere people interact with your brand such as marketing materials, LinkedIn profile, website, bio, etc.

THE 3 C'S OF COACHING

Recall in "Chapter 1: Coach Stories," we introduced you to "The 3 C's of Coaching:"

#1: Coach what you know: Your background and experience.

#2: Combine what you know with your abilities: Your background aligned with your strengths and skills.

#3: Care deeply about the work: Your motivation.

I will walk you through the following exercises to help you identify your background experiences (what you know), to integrate your abilities you've identified ("Strengths" and "Skills" exercises from earlier in this chapter), and to identify your motivation for who you want to help.

#1: Coach what you know: Your background and experience

If you have experience other than coaching, what roles or industries did you work in? That is low-hanging fruit for you to target those people. Your religion, background, and the area you're from are all part of your story.

Michelle Rademacher transitioned from a career as an architect to recruiting. Upon leaving recruiting to start her coaching business, she initially targeted architects who looked to transition careers. She understood their work on a personal level and had successfully transitioned her own career which supplied instant credibility.

In other examples, I met a coach who reads romance novels and decided to create group coaching using romance novels as the centerpiece of discussions. I've met military spouses-turned-coaches who found themselves in a job search every three years when their spouses were deployed to a new location. They understand the unique challenges of the situation.

Coach what you know, whether that's through group identification, geography, or shared experiences.

ACTIVITY:

Choose themes from your background or experiences and bullet key elements of your story.

Do you have a background in start-ups or the non-profit sector? Do you have experience in particular industries? What communities do you belong to? Examples are homeschool groups, military veteran groups, parenting groups, faith-based communities, clubs, etc. Next, what experience do you have? Do you have experience managing people, teaching, supporting customers, launching programs, creating processes, or community outreach?

For example, I worked in the S.T.E.M. field (Science, Technology, Engineering, Math) for 11 years. I could highlight my experiences to help women working in

S.T.E.M. fields to negotiate salary or raises, bring a diverse and unique perspective to problem solving, and successfully pitch ideas. Add your keywords and bulleted items from the activity to the "My Background/Experience" section of your *Coach Canvas*. The example in "The Coach Canvas" section at the beginning of this chapter is:

My Background/Experience

Industries: Healthcare, Education, Training, Coaching

Roles: Operations Management, L&D Leadership

#2: Combine what you know with your abilities: Your background aligned with your strengths and skills

If you have completed *The Four Pillars of Career Fit*™ exercises in this chapter, you have the data for this step: your strengths and skills. You were prompted to add both of these to your *Coach Canvas* in the *Appendix*. If you have not completed "Pillar One: My Strengths" and "Pillar Three: My Skills," that is your starting point.

In the previous activity, you listed aspects of your background and experiences. What expertise do you have and how can you marry this experience with your strengths and skills?

For example, let's say a person has experience working in a small startup and was responsible for creating processes. In addition, he has the *Strategic, Discipline* and *Arranger* strengths. Along with his strengths, his top skills are managing logistics, planning, organizing, and mentoring.

This blend of experiences and abilities would be well-suited to consulting with startup founders to help them establish processes that scale as his or her company grows. The goal of these exercises is to inventory your experiences, strengths, and skills, then think of ways to integrate them. This will bring focus on who you can help and services you could offer. Building upon your background and abilities can only increase your credibility.

Even if you didn't enjoy the experiences you had, coaching or consulting others in those areas will feel different than performing the duties yourself. You might enjoy mentoring, coaching, teaching and training related to your background more than you enjoyed performing the tasks.

✎ ACTIVITY:

Reflect: How do your experiences and abilities add value to clients? If you've done CliftonStrengths, download your *Strengths Insight Guide* at gallup.com/cliftonstrengths. Your personalized report is filled with story prompts. This exercise can also provide insight to allow you to complete "Who I Help" in your *Coach Canvas*. That is the next activity.

_____

_____

_____

_____

_____

_____

#3: Care deeply about the work: Your motivation

Your why and your purpose will attract different people. Why do you want to work with certain clients, such as students, recent retirees, women leaders, people recently released from prison, men in at-risk industries who want to transition, executives, etc.?

What drives you about the work you
do and for whom you do it?

Laura (not her real name) is a successful, well-regarded coach who works with women executives at a Fortune 100 ranked company. She does her job well and leaders get better results after working with her. I was speaking with Laura on the phone and she asked me, "Why do I feel like something is missing in my career?"

Laura had made it to the top as a coach yet still felt a void. We went over her values, and I pointed out that "making a difference" and "meaningful work" are both in her top ten values. She knows she makes a difference coaching women in the corporate arena, but what was missing was deep meaning.

Making a difference impacts others. It's outside of us. Meaningful work is internal to us. We can volunteer or engage in activities that help others and make a significant impact, but those contributions might not be what we consider most meaningful.

When Laura and I shifted to who she feels led to help, she kept coming back to disadvantaged women and girls. We discussed how she could balance her executive client load to make room for non-profit coaching and laid out potential future paths, such as an Executive Director role within a non-profit primarily focused on helping her target population, or training coaches to support her own non-profit initiative, where she would also continue to coach.

Money is not Laura's primary motivation. She is driven to be an advocate, using creativity and resourcefulness to help others find fulfillment. Acknowledging her values gave Laura the confirmation she needed to pursue work more closely aligned to what mattered most to her.

 ACTIVITY:

What do you care deeply about? *Why?*

Who are you motivated to help, or whose challenges often cross your mind?

List groups or individuals you have experience helping, paid or unpaid, in the space provided. Experience with a population isn't always required, but it's nice to have. Which of these individuals or groups provide the motivation you're looking for?

Add individuals or groups you are motivated to help into the "Who I Help" section of your *Coach Canvas*.

_____

_____

_____

_____

_____

_____

_____

_____

THE ROLE OF A COACH

In "Chapter 1: Coach Stories," Judi introduced you to her philosophy: the role of a coach is to encourage a person about his or her situation and move that person to action.

As a coach, you should seek to become clear on the answer to these two questions:

How can I encourage this person?

How can I move this person to action?

As mentioned in the previous chapter, there are a multitude of ways to encourage a person and move that person to action. Your approach lies in your abilities. I've listed a handful of strengths below and how they might help you as a coach to encourage or move people to action. If this seems self-explanatory, skip past the list of examples and begin the exercise. If you're uncertain and need more clarification, review the examples.

How I Encourage People

Adaptability – Flexible, easy to talk to and get along with

Analytical – Logical, rigorous, able to think through factors to bring a realistic and grounded perspective

Communication – Able to inspire people with words and storytelling

Connectedness – Give people hope, help others see the big picture and that there are no coincidences

Empathy – Able to hear unvoiced needs

Futuristic – Inspire others with a vision for the future

Individualization – See people's strengths and draw the best out of them

Positivity – Encourage and fuel optimism

Relator – Seek to understand feelings, goals and dreams

Restorative – Able to quickly pinpoint the root of a problem

Activator – Create enthusiasm and a sense of urgency to turn thoughts into action

Arranger – Find the most efficient and productive way to get things done

Developer – Stretch people to their potential to help them grow

Discipline – Adept at creating plans of action, break plans into manageable steps

Focus – Able to pinpoint priorities, set goals, and act on those goals

Input – Provide resources and resourcefulness to help clients with problem solving, decision-making, planning, and more

Responsibility – Model accountability

Strategic – Determine the best path forward when faced with multiple options

ACTIVITY:

List your strengths from your *Coach Canvas* in the space provided and consider how you encourage and move others to action. Choose at least one strength for encouraging, and one for moving others to action. Download your personalized *Strengths Insight Guide* at gallup.com/cliftonstrengths to simplify the activity. Craft a brief statement to add into the "How I Encourage Clients" section of the *Coach Canvas* in the *Appendix*. Then craft and add a brief statement into the section "How I Move Them to Action" in the *Coach Canvas*.

_____

_____

_____

_____

_____

_____

_____

_____

No one delivers the exact contribution you do. Your unique experiences combine with your unique design to deliver a unique offering. Let's figure out what that is!

You will have a lot of data after completing *The Four Pillars of Career Fit*™ exercises. Review your *Coach Canvas* and highlight the words and phrases that resonate most with you.

Below you will find a link to a video to walk you through creation of a "Unique Contribution Statement" that you can add to your *Coach Canvas*. In the video, I demonstrate how to create your statement using my *Four Pillars of Career Fit*™ framework (strengths, values, skills, and personality-based interests). The video will guide you to build a statement based on keywords in your *Coach Canvas*.

Consider using a less common word (not jargon) to grab the reader's attention. I will share ideas for using your statement in the next "Idea for Action" following the exercise.

---

bit.ly/UCStatementTutorial
(URL is case-sensitive)

ACTIVITY:
    List your keywords in the space provided as you work through the video.

Draft your "My Unique Contribution" statement using some of the keywords you selected. Share your statement with people who know you for feedback, then add it to your *Coach Canvas*.

_____

_____

_____

_____

_____

_____

_____

_____

Idea for Action *Communicate Your Unique Contribution Statement*

Write brief stories using your statement as a prompt. The stories should incorporate elements from your statement to illustrate your unique contribution to others.

Share relevant stories with prospective clients in discovery calls, preferably no more than two minutes in length. Expand the stories into videos for your website, blogs and social media posts.

Share your favorite story as an accomplishment within your LinkedIn summary. If you have a website, you can better align your website content with your *My Unique Contribution* through the stories you tell and the testimonials you share.

After completing the exercises, you'll have a clear picture of yourself. The *Coach Canvas* will help you see patterns and themes.

How does the story within your Coach Canvas align with what clients or colleagues say about you?

To avoid disrupting your flow completing the exercises, I waited to share deeper insight into *The Four Pillars of Career Fit™*. *Strengths, values, skills,* and *personality-based interests* interact with one another. Additional powerful insights about you or your clients come to light through these interactions.

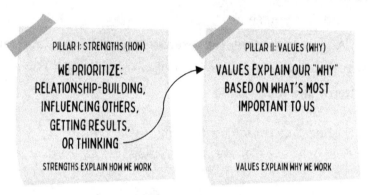

Priorities are expressed through *values*

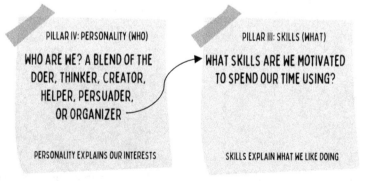

Personality-based *interests* are expressed through *skills*

© YouMap LLC

Refer to the top half of the previous image. Our *strengths* set our priorities. Our *priorities* are then expressed through our *values*. Let me clarify this concept with an example.

Recall, people have one or more of the four main priorities:

Relationship-building

Influencing Others

Getting Results

Thinking

If you have *relationship-building* strengths, *how* you work is by building meaningful relationships. Relationships would be your priority. If you had *result-oriented* strengths, getting things done would be a greater priority than building relationships.

You can have one or more of the four priorities. My priorities are *influencing* and *thinking* which is why I write books. One of my top values is making a difference. I want to influence people for their greater good by writing books that I hope will make a difference.

Think about your strengths and values. Can you come up with examples of your strengths expressing through your values? If this isn't quite clear yet, my friend and coach Loreen Marshall's example should bring this concept to life. Then you can give it another try. If you don't need an example, skip to the next section, "Interests Are Expressed Through Skills."

Loreen's priority is *relationship-building*. Her top five values are:

Love/connection, making a difference, generosity, fun, and flexibility.

Loreen expresses her *relationship-building* priority through these values. In relationships, she craves quality time with the people in her life (love/connection). An example is throwing backyard summer parties for friends and family.

Loreen wants to help make people's lives better. She supports a non-profit organization, *Friends of Padhar Schools,* which helps schools in Padhar, India and surrounding villages (making a difference).

Loreen shares her resources with others (generosity). One example is her time. Loreen is a beta-reader of both my adult and children's books and offers exceptional feedback.

Loreen enjoys laughing with people she cares about and hosts monthly Bunco game nights (fun).

Lastly, Loreen goes out of her way help friends (flexibility). She once drove an hour and a half roundtrip to bring a manuscript to my house so I would get it faster than if she had mailed it.

Loreen is fabulous, and I have language to explain *how* and *why* she's fabulous by illustrating how her priorities are expressed through her values.

Refer to the "Strengths" and "Top Values" sections on your *Coach Canvas*. Write how *your* strengths express through your values:

1. _____

2. _____

3. _____

4. _____

5. _____

INTERESTS ARE EXPRESSED THROUGH SKILLS

Refer to the bottom half of the last graphic shown. Your *personality* influences your *interests*. Your *interests* are then expressed through your *skills*. Let's look at an example for this concept, as well.

Recall that we discussed earlier in the chapter that people have a blend (usually we choose the top two) of the following personality-based interests:

Doer

Thinker

Creator

Persuader

Helper

Organizer

I mentioned earlier in this chapter that interests are a stronger predictor of vocational choice than standard personality assessments like DISC, Big Five, and MBTI.

Judi: As I share the following story, keep in mind that my top interest types are the **persuader**, **creator**, *and* **organizer**.

The summer I was expecting Kristin, I was as big as a house and it was really hot. I would spend my days at my sister Rhoda's house in her pool because it was the only place I was comfortable.

When I wasn't in the pool, I was on the deck reading a book. So, picture this. I was a 25-year-old stay-at-home mom. I had Kristin's five-year-old brother Wayne, and I was a high school dropout. The book I was reading was called Up the Organization by Robert Townsend. It was a book on Organizational Development. As I read the book, I thought about how much I would love doing that work — the work I do today.

That was 10 years before I went to college and 25 years before I started graduate school. And what else was I doing at that time? I was baking pies and making biscuits. I would cut out pictures from magazines and tell my husband I would love to build a house. He thought the idea was crazy. We've now done that three times.

Baking and homebuilding have something in common. They are both a combination of **creator** *and* **organizer**. *And talking my husband into building a house three separate times leaned heavily on* **persuader**!

In hindsight, you can see the **persuader**, *the* **creator**, *and the* **organizer** *within me at twenty-five.*

Now, let's look at how personality-based interests express through skills. My preferred skill categories are leadership, conceptual/creative, research/analysis, and interpersonal. My specific preferred skills from my YouMap® are in bold text.

Judi's Preferred Skills

Administration:	Leadership:	Sales:
Budget	**Initiate Change**	Competitiveness
Categorize	**Lead Others**	Negotiate
Organize	**Mentor**	**Present/Perform**
Paperwork	**Motivate**	Risk Taking
		Sell

Conceptual/Creative:	Manage:	Supervise:
Abstract Thinking	Process/Projects	**Decision Making**
Ambiguity, Deal w/	Customer Service	**Delegate**
Create Images	Execute	Hiring/Staffing
Design	Handle Change	Manage Others
Envision	Manage Logistics	
Ideate	Manage Time	
Improvise	Monitor	
Innovate	Multi-Task	
Strategize	Plan	

Interpersonal:	Research/ Analysis:	Technical/Mechanical:
Advise	**Analyze**	Computer Skills
Collaborate	**Assess**	**Edit**
Instruct/Train	**Interview for**	Estimate
Liaise	**Information**	Mechanical
Manage Emotions	**Observe**	Numeric Accuracy
Mediate	**Research**	**Test**
Use Intuition	Study	**Write**

As an executive coach, my interest types are fully used. Clients hire me to help them with large, complex projects that require a systematic approach (organizer). I have created over one hundred processes and tools to support these large projects (creator).

Whether I am coaching or consulting with executive level individuals, I need to influence to be effective (persuader). All three of my interest types express through my preferred skills.

For example, I persuade through the instruct/train skill when I lead workshops. I also persuade through the present/perform skill when I deliver a talk.

My organizer interest often expresses through the skills of analyze, assess, interview for information, observe, and research. Organizations expect process and data-driven approaches. I naturally approach engagements with process and structure because of my organizer interest type. The process is data-driven because I have a preference for research and analysis skills.

These interests showed up early in my life and have only gotten stronger over time. Knowing what skills to hone based on your interests is powerful information for you and your clients.

Refer to the "Top 5 Skills" and "Interests" sections on your *Coach Canvas*. Write how *your* interests express through your top five skills:

1. _____

2. _____

3. _____

4. _____

5. _____

In "Chapter 1: Coach Stories," Judi shared "The 3 C's of Coaching:" coach what you know, combine what you know with your talents, and care deeply about the work. How you work with clients to leverage your experience, abilities, and interests is an important consideration.

Based on experiences working with coaches and consultants one-on-one and in group training, I have discovered some people coach but are better suited for consulting. Others are consulting and would get more satisfaction coaching. Some practitioners would benefit most by offering a hybrid model of coaching and consulting.

How can you tell if coaching, consulting, or a hybrid approach is best suited for you? Let's move to the next chapter to work through the answer to this question.

3

COACH OR CONSULTANT?
Kristin

Coach and consultant are not the same role. A core distinction between the role of coach and consultant is *where power lives.*

Coaches are a "guide on the side." A good coach is seen as a source of wisdom and will seek the truth along with clients to help them find it. A consultant offers the solutions a client needs to solve problems or get results.

In other words, consultants are paid for the expertise they possess. A coach might have expertise but the process, guidance through questions and stories and accountability offered throughout that process, is central to the value a coach brings.

There are exceptions to this delineation in the coaching world. One example is in sports. Athletic coaches tend to have more power than the athletes, in many cases to an authoritarian extent.

One of the first decisions you should make is if you want to coach, consult, or offer a hybrid model of coaching and consulting. For example, you might coach individual clients to help them get unstuck in a particular area of life. Let's say you ask questions to help clarify the problem, aid your client in setting goals, and help her think through how she might tackle each goal. Finally, you supply accountability through monthly touch-base meetings as she works toward each goal. In this example you are *coaching*.

In addition to coaching, you might also offer strategy sessions where clients share a particular problem and you design a solution based on your expertise. In this example you are *consulting*.

Judi and I have different businesses. I have shifted from coaching individual career changers to a hybrid of training and consulting for coaches, many of whom are self-employed or have a side hustle. Judi also employs a hybrid approach of coaching and consulting but works with leaders and their teams in organizations.

Clients will sometimes ask Judi's opinion, even when she is coaching, because of her specific experience. She uses this opportunity to tell clients a story that has a moral embedded in it related to their issue. Then they can decide what they want to do after they've heard the story.

Judi: An example of employing a hybrid approach occurred when I was coaching a newly promoted plant manager who received a call from corporate headquarters. An outside contract manufacturer was interested in bidding on my client's biggest product that was currently manufactured in-house. Seventy percent of their manufacturing resources were dedicated to this product.

The contract manufacturer was willing to produce the product at a significant discount. Corporate accepting this offer could have shuttered the facility. My client had two choices. He could make the decision himself and send a new proposal, or he could work with his direct reports' departments and ask them to shape a proposal. He chose the latter but just in case, calculated preliminary figures independently.

After meeting with his direct reports' departments and explaining the problem, he gave them a week to produce a solution that would prevent their facility from being closed down. The solutions proposed by his direct reports were better than the solution he was considering.

I will sometimes share stories like this one with other new managers when asked my opinion when they are facing their first big decision. The moral of this story is don't be afraid to reach out to the expertise of people you work with, regardless of their level in the organization. The tendency of new leaders is to think they need to have all the answers. A leader's direct reports are often closer to opportunities than the executives. A story like this helps my clients make their own decisions based on experiences I share with them.

You don't have to guess if coaching or consulting is best for you. I will refer back to *The Four Pillars of Career Fit*™ introduced in the last chapter and walk you through *A Tale of Two Coaches*. The examples of two real coaches will illustrate how these pillars can help you decide on coaching versus consulting and build a practice that feels energizing.

I've worked with coaches on the verge of folding their business and quitting coaching. After a conversation, I was able to help these coaches discover the root problem and help them renew their focus. *The Four Pillars of Career Fit*™ have not yet failed to reveal the problem(s) behind career dissatisfaction.

How do *The Four Pillars of Career Fit*™ influence fit as a coach versus a consultant? Let's take a deeper look and then you'll have a chance to work through a coach versus consultant exercise to apply the information to yourself.

A TALE OF TWO COACHES

Susan's Story

In early 2021, I had a conversation with Susan (not her real name). She had started a coaching practice and in less than two years was thinking about calling it quits. I've seen similar situations where coaches are excited to start their own practice only to discover they don't like what they're doing. Several causes might explain this unexpected change of heart:

- Consulting is a better fit than coaching
- Low priority skills take up too much of your day
- Service offerings, or the execution, are a poor fit for a person's strengths, values, skills, or personality
- You're serving the wrong clients

In Susan's case, all these causes were an issue.

Susan was offering coaching services, and while the clients were different, the problems the clients had were always the same. As she shared her dissatisfaction and that she was thinking of closing her business, I said to her, "From what I've heard you say, it sounds like you're bored with your work and not sufficiently challenged. Is that correct?"

She responded as if what I said was a revelation. To me, it wasn't revelatory at all, but sometimes we're just too close to ourselves to see things clearly. You see, there were things I knew about Susan that made it easy for me to connect the dots about what wasn't working.

Since Susan had recently gone through certification with me hoping to gain renewed interest in her business, I could quickly scroll through her assessment data as she shared her concerns.

Let's use *The Four Pillars of Career Fit*™ (strengths, values, skills, and personality-based interests) to explain why Susan, the coach, felt bored and unchallenged in her business.

Susan's "how" (strengths):
- Curious, resourceful, wants intellectual stimulation
- Learner, enjoys sharing those learnings with others
- Enjoys meeting new people
- Helps people connect their dots and find purpose
- Achiever who works hard and wants results

As a reminder, Susan was delivering career coaching services such as resume writing and job search coaching. When you read Susan's priorities above, why do you think I concluded she was bored? She was living the same day every day. She met new people, but the client needs and service delivery became routine.

How Susan Works (Strengths)

Susan was missing complex mental challenges. Three of her five strengths are in the *thinking* and *executing* domain. Because she is curious, resourceful, and connects dots others miss, she would experience satisfaction helping people solve challenges. Each situation would differ and offer a mental challenge, resulting in sustained interest. Susan does have two *relationship-building* strengths and would still be working with people, but *solutions* would be the focal point, not the person, as with coaching.

Who is Susan? (Personality-based interests)

Recall the six Holland types: *doer*, *thinker*, *creator*, *helper*, *persuader*, and *organizer*. Susan's personality type is the *helper* and the *thinker*, known as The Specialist. Here is a snippet from The Specialist description:

> The Specialist seeks a purposeful career, usually in a helping profession. They do not enjoy simply socializing with people but want to learn about them in a way that supplies intellectual stimulation. The Specialist combines an ardent desire to help people with

the intellectual curiosity and ability to do so in ways most people can't. (source: Susan's YouMap® profile)

When I discussed The Specialist with Susan, it strongly resonated. Helping people through coaching wasn't enough. She needs to help people *by deeply engaging her brain*. It was yet another indication Susan should focus on helping others through expertise. At the start of this chapter, I mentioned that consultants are paid for the *expertise* they possess. We could walk through her values and skills to find further evidence why consulting is a better fit, but I hope you get the idea based on her strengths and personality.

Cristina's Story

I worked with Cristina in 2020. As she took steps to begin coaching, she felt unsure about working one-on-one with clients or running coaching groups.

As she thought about group coaching, something didn't feel right. Yet, when she thought about coaching one-on-one, something also felt missing. What a conundrum! Yet her reaction is easily explained.

Following are Cristina's strengths, the first pillar of *The Four Pillars of Fit*™ (drawn from the 34 CliftonStrengths that can be found in the *Appendix*):

Activator (influencing) – Makes things happen by turning thoughts into actions.

Connectedness (relationship-building) – Bridge-builder

who sees the big picture and helps others see purpose.

Developer (relationship-building) – Recognizes and cultivates potential in others.

WOO (influencing) – Loves the challenge of meeting new people and "winning others over."

Arranger (executing) – Organizes, yet also has a flexibility that complements this ability. They like to figure out how all the pieces and resources can be arranged for maximum productivity.

Notice Cristina has *relationship-building* strengths which lean toward deeper one-on-one connections. She also has *influencing* strengths that indicate she enjoys meeting new people and prioritizes influencing others to action.

Straddling both *relationship-building* and *influencing* strengths explains why she felt pulled toward one-on-one and group coaching, while also feeling something was missing from each!

Specifically, since Cristina has the *Connectedness (relationship-building)* strength, she felt she would not connect deeply enough with participants in a group setting.

To resolve this problem, I encouraged Cristina to create a hybrid coaching program. If she structured the program to include group *and* one-on-one coaching, she could conduct one-on-one private sessions with each group member. Her pricing strategy should take the added individualized attention into account.

This hybrid solution is not only favorable for Cristina but for clients. The group aspect supplies a support network for participants as well as a more affordable price point than one-on-one coaching. The one-one-one aspect offers personalized attention. If Cristina keeps the group limited to five or six people, she can offer engaging group interactions supplemented with deeper personalization.

Regardless of how Cristina structures her program, she is a coach through and through. Consulting would not interest her because she is focused on people. Four of her top five strengths are people-oriented and none of them are in the *thinking* domain. I expect to see at least one *thinking* strength in someone interested in consulting.

Hopefully these stories brought *The Four Pillars of Career Fit*™ to life and got you thinking about a preference for coaching, consulting, or a hybrid solution. Now let's talk about you.

DO YOU PREFER COACHING OR CONSULTING?

Ultimately, the decision to coach, consult, or offer a hybrid model of services is your decision. What I'm about to share isn't prescriptive. Trust what you know about yourself along with what you have learned through the exercises in the book.

In general, I have observed a few patterns working with coaches:

1. People with *relationship-building* strengths often

prefer one-on-one coaching over group coaching. Relationship-builders tend to be more comfortable working with one person over a longer period, such as six to twelve months.

2. Individuals with *influencing* strengths tend to prefer consulting, group coaching, training, workshops, or shorter engagements where individual clients rotate in and out quickly, or they have an opportunity to coach a variety of people within an organization rather than prolonged coaching engagements with individuals.

3. People with a mix of *influencing* and *relationship-building* strengths sometimes choose a blend of coaching and consulting because they enjoy what both experiences offer. Sometimes they want to work one-on-one and go deeper with an individual, while other times they enjoy the leadership and influence of consulting. A hybrid approach can offer the variety this blend needs. Keep in mind, *thinking* strengths are an advantage when working as a consultant.

4. People with a combination of *thinking, influencing,* or *executing* strengths tend to prefer consulting over coaching. *Relationship-building* focuses on people. Task-oriented people, such as those with combined *thinking, influencing, and executing* strengths, are focused on problems and solutions.

Examples of consulting:

Strategy consulting

Marketing consulting

Operations consulting

Financial consulting

Human Resources consulting

Compliance consulting

Technology/IT consulting

Legal consulting

Sales consulting

Environmental/sustainability consulting

Growth marketing consulting

Public Relations consulting

Examples of coaching:

Behavior adaptation

High performance/high potential

Intervention

Skill development

Goal setting and accountability

Mindset and mindfulness

Job performance

Career transition/General career coaching

Team-building

Grief recovery

Personal training or weight loss

Do you feel a pull to one of these lists more than the other, or toward both?

Review your *Coach Canvas* and observe the *pattern* of your data. Does your canvas read like a coach with strengths, values, skills, interests, and traits associated with deeper, one-on-one connections? Does your canvas reveal a blend of *influencing* and *thinking* that sounds more like consulting? Do you notice elements of both, which might point to an interest in a hybrid approach of consulting and coaching?

My grandmother used to say a problem identified is half solved. Sometimes a solution is just a few tweaks away. If you start to sense burn out, lack of engagement or motivation, or something isn't right that you can't put your finger on, consider:

Are you consulting or coaching?

How are you offering and delivering services?

Who are you working with?

What skills are you using daily?

How interested are you in what you're doing?

Periodically assess alignment to your strengths, values, preferred skills, and personality-based interests. *The Four Pillars of Career Fit*™ hold many answers to explain your dissatisfaction.

Let's build upon what you've learned in this chapter and extend it to identifying your ideal clients.

4

YOUR IDEAL CLIENTS
Kristin

Discovering your ideal clients takes mindful effort. Working through the steps to make sure you're attracting and choosing the right customers is time well spent.

As you consider what you do best that your clients need most, remember that not all clients are good clients. We'll discuss how to conduct effective prospect calls in Part III of the book, but we'd like you to keep the following graphic in mind.

WHAT RESULT DOES THE CLIENT WANT?
DO THEY...

KNOW WHAT THEY WANT?

NOT KNOW WHAT THEY WANT?

TRUST YOU?

DISTRUST YOU?

You will come across four kinds of prospective clients:

#1

Client doesn't know what they want

+

Client doesn't trust you

Your prospect knows they are stuck or not moving toward a goal. Your prospect doesn't know what the goal should be. You might be uncertain if they lack trust in your competence, or if they don't trust you will deliver something they actually want or need. You might even sense you must prove yourself during the conversation.

This is someone you will regret engaging as a client.

Listen to your gut! Avoid working with clients who don't trust you, as this situation will likely not benefit either of you. It could also take a negative turn such as the client demanding a refund, writing a negative review of your services, or approaching you with skepticism throughout the time you work together.

Instead, refer the prospect to another resource or a coach who may be a better fit. Explain that coaching is a personal and trusted relationship and you don't sense you are the right coach for them.

#2

Client doesn't know what they want

+

Client trusts you

The prospect might trust you based on your content on social media or a referral from a mutual friend. Perhaps you simply hit it off on an initial call. A client doesn't necessarily have to be clear on what they want. If they trust you to help them get clear and move forward, that is a win/win. Clients that don't know what they want but trust you to help them figure it out can be phenomenal ambassadors of your work if you have facilitated a breakthrough for them.

This is a client you will want to work with.

One warning to note: If the coaching services you offer are dependent on client clarity, such as job search strategy coaching, this client might not be a good fit. If that's the case, explain what they need to do first before they are ready to work with you, or refer them to someone in your network who helps people in the phase the prospect is in.

#3

Client knows what they want

+

Client doesn't trust you

If a client is clear on their goal but skeptical of you as a coach, this is unlikely to be a good client. They're not going to hire you and that's a good thing! Who wants to jump through hoops to try to convince a person you know what you're doing?

This is someone you will regret engaging as a client.

As previously mentioned, you can refer the prospective client to another resource or coach who is a better fit. Explain that coaching is a personal and trusted relationship and you don't sense you are the best fit to work together.

Perhaps offer a bit of parting guidance to help them take the next step about who to work with or what to focus on.

#4

Client knows what they want

+

Client trusts you

The client knows what they want and they trust you can guide them to that result. This is what you want to be looking for in your prospect calls as it is the ideal scenario. They are clear on their goal, they are clear on the services you offer, and they have faith in you as a coach to guide them.

This is a client you will want to work with.

In addition to evaluating clients on the above dimensions, don't underestimate your gut instinct. When your gut tells you to run and you're still tempted to engage with a prospect remember the six words, "Not all clients are good clients."

I now train coaches, but when I was coaching individuals, most clients were referrals. A past client referred a woman to me who had a college-aged daughter needing guidance for her career path.

Often when a prospective client emailed me, I offered a discovery call to figure out if we were a good fit to work together, both as individuals and in the services I offered. Prior to a call, the prospective client's mother sent me a number of questions by email.

She requested a variety of data and metrics to prove her daughter would get satisfactory results if she worked with me. I didn't have an issue with being asked about my results, but something didn't feel right, as if I had to jump through hoops despite referral by a customer who raved about our coaching engagement.

The mother was skeptical by nature, so I understood her caution and didn't take it personally. We all have unique needs, preferences, and motivations based on our personality and priorities.

The testimonials of my clients have always spoken for me. So, when a customer's referral wasn't sufficient for the prospective client to trust me, I knew I would not take on this client because she fell into client type number three (client knows what they want + client doesn't trust you). I value being a trusted expert in my field and trying to persuade or prove I could help her didn't feel authentic for me.

I responded to her request explaining that coaching is a deeply personal relationship. It's important she, and her daughter, hire a coach they fully trust. I recommended they seek a coach in whom they could place complete confidence and wished her daughter every success. I never received a reply.

I try to avoid making assumptions that she was displeased about being preemptively fired as my client. Yet, it did give me the feeling I made the right call. No one ever says, "I wish I never listened to my gut."

Most of us can figure out a client isn't a fit once we're already working with them, but how do you find out *before* they hire you? In addition to following the guidelines above, let's build your ideal client profile.

Build Your Ideal Client Profile

During a career coaching engagement, I was helping an executive in transition. Peter had been a vice president in Fortune 500 companies as well as an executive in a startup, building a 900M business.

He was searching for clarity on rejoining a large company, becoming a consultant, or teaching in a university. We found consulting was the best fit for his desire to do what he wanted, when he wanted, from wherever he wanted.

My client had a clear understanding of his values, but had never connected those values to the characteristics of clients he wanted to attract. He completed the following exercise, and his results are below. I invite you to do the same in the space provided below his example.

Qualities Of High Value Clients & Obstacles to Success

Traits or qualities of Peter's high value clients:

- Trust
- Mutual respect
- Open Communication
- Committed to a common agenda

Obstacles to success for Peter's clients:

- Disengaged client
- Lacks clarity on what's most important

- Focused on less critical issues
- Prematurely moves to action
- Doesn't recognize Peter's value
- Uncommitted to personal mastery

Think back to early communications with your difficult clients. What themes occurred? Were there early warning signs or red flags? Did the client show particular behaviors or communication patterns?

As an example, when I was coaching, I didn't enjoy working with people who had a scarcity mindset, made excuses, or shot down ideas without a willingness to try. In prospect calls, I paid close attention to the language potential clients used. Red flags deterred me from working with a prospect. Warning signs included:

- "The problem is…"
- Cant's and buts
- Victim mentality
- "That won't work because…"
- Lack of enthusiasm for working together
- Overt negativity
- Excuses and lack of accountability
- Lack of commitment

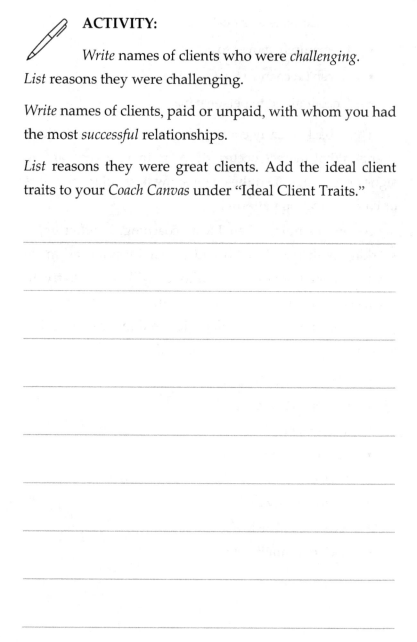

ACTIVITY:

Write names of clients who were *challenging*. *List* reasons they were challenging.

Write names of clients, paid or unpaid, with whom you had the most *successful* relationships.

List reasons they were great clients. Add the ideal client traits to your *Coach Canvas* under "Ideal Client Traits."

Do you ask your best clients at the end of coaching if they know people like them who need your help? Birds of a feather flock together.

You have a unique coaching style because you are a unique individual. When you are keenly aware of certain factors about yourself, it enables you to clearly understand who you are as a coach and how you affect your clients. You will also gain more insight into who you will enjoy serving most as a coach.

Think about how the factors that make you unique could create an advantage for your clients that they're unlikely to receive from coaches who don't have your unique characteristics. This sort of reflection helps you uncover what you do best that others need most.

YOUR IMMEDIATE NETWORK

If you haven't worked with clients, it can be hard to know who you will work well with and who you won't. Your first step is to explore and test. Start working with people to get a feel for who you enjoy working with.

One great place to test drive clients is in your immediate network. Who knows you by first name, engages with you online, or lives near you? Connect with people in your network and let them know the exciting ways you're now helping people solve problems and get the results they want. If people in your network don't have a current need for your services, maybe they know someone who does.

When they talk to people who need your help, you will come to mind. You probably have a larger network than you might think.

ACTIVITY:

List specific people you can think of who could be helped by your services or products, including people you've helped who might welcome being an ambassador.

Why might they be interested?

Examples are people with whom you volunteer, share hobbies, or go to church. Others include alumni or professors from your academic institution, past or present coworkers you trust, friends and extended family, fellow members of professional associations or clubs, mentors or business contacts, former and current clients.

_____

_____

_____

_____

_____

_____

Focus on the interests of the person with whom you are communicating. At the center should be their needs and your desire to help, rather than what you want.

Say this…	Instead of this…
You deserve fulfillment in your career. That's why our system focuses on helping you make better career decisions.	**We** have a proven career system with one goal in mind: helping clients make better decisions.

Dale Carnegie, an expert in relationship advice, sums it up in the following quote:

> *"You can make more friends in two months by becoming interested in other people than you can in two years by trying to get other people interested in you."* – *Dale Carnegie*

I come across a lot of "I'm so excited to tell you about my new book" posts on a regular basis on social media. Posts begin with enthusiasm of the accomplishment, an explanation of the arduous work that went into it, oftentimes the people who made it possible, followed by "if you buy my book I'd be grateful."

The problem is few people care. I wish it weren't true. We want to believe we care. In a noisy, information-overloaded world, we have competition for our attention. Our brains filter out most things that don't relate to us to avoid overstimulating and overwhelming our brains.

To get the people in your network to care about what you have to say, they need to see quickly and clearly what your message is about and, more importantly, how they will benefit if they pay attention. One effective approach is to ask questions and listen intently to the answers. An example will drive this point home.

If you call, write, or interact with a family friend online, and this friend has a son graduating from high school, you might ask, "Has Miguel decided on a college major? If he feels overwhelmed or a bit lost, please call me. Eighty percent of college students change their major an average of three times. I can help save him that frustration."

The principle of your message focusing on the other person is true for social media content, too. Following is a social media post, de-identified to protect the innocent, and summarized for brevity without removing any themes:

> I'm excited to announce that my new book [Book Title] is finally out! It's been an amazing journey to get this book published, and I'm thrilled to share it with you.
>
> This book would never have happened without the help of so many people.
>
> [Twenty-six people were then tagged and thanked here. People you've never heard of and don't care about].
>
> Download a free chapter here. If you like it, buy the book here. And if you really like it, please write a review because reviews help.

Were you intrigued or moved by this post?

Focus on the interests of the person with whom you are communicating. At the center should be their needs and your desire to help, rather than what you want.

CLIENT-ALIGNED VALUES

In "Chapter 2: You, the Coach," you were presented with exercises to uncover *The Four Pillars of Career Fit*™. Your values is one of the pillars. Values are critically important to work with the right clients. *It feels different to coach, and to be coached by, people with different values.* For example, imagine a coach values knowledge, expertise, status, and authority. The client values connection, collaboration, authenticity, and humility. The coach and the client might place importance and focus on different things and fail to experience a trusted connection.

Use the language of your values and the impact you want to have in your marketing material, social media profiles, social media content, conversations, and prospecting calls. You will attract people who click with your values.

For example, if you value *responsibility*, clients who cancel appointments, don't complete coaching exercises, or lack commitment will frustrate you. Speak your values to attract like-minded clients. For example, "I help career changers who want to take responsibility for driving their career but are uncertain of their next career move."

Stating your values will influence clients to opt in or out of working with you based on how connected and aligned they are to the values statements in your marketing.

Speak your values to attract like-minded clients.

Fun is one of my values. Whether I am speaking, training, or coaching, I like to inject fun into the experience. Seeing smiles across the audience in response to an amusing story is energizing. On the other hand, coaching or training people who are disengaged because they were forced to be there is a total bummer, which affects my energy in the opposite direction.

Several years ago, I was facilitating a strength workshop with the sales team for a video game company in California. Coaching clients in the gaming industry was new for me and I was excited for the opportunity. My enthusiasm was short-lived.

It became clear at the outset that the manager was committed to team strengths exploration, but the team did not buy into the workshop. Before we even began, the participants were distracted, disengaged, and even occasionally disruptive. The team did not appear to value personal growth or self-discovery, making the experience one that I never care to repeat.

In hindsight, I should have asked questions up-front about the team, goals for participating in the workshop, and what communications had occurred to set expectations. If none of these steps had been taken, I would have offered a brief expectation-setting meeting to generate interest in how the session could benefit each individual and the group as a whole.

Discovering your values will spare aggravation when working with clients. Values exploration is something you should consider incorporating into your client coaching process, as well, depending on the kind of work you do. Values affect every area of our life.

MANAGING DIFFICULT CLIENTS

Congratulations! You've done the work. You know your strengths, values, preferred skills, your personality, motivation, the problems you solve, the solutions you offer, traits of your ideal clients, who your high value partners are, your story to attract those clients and partners, and you can articulate your unique contribution.

Despite all that effort, somehow, you end up with a challenging client. You took too much cold medicine before the discovery call and missed the red flags. The client was your best friend's cousin's daughter and you didn't have the heart to say no.

No matter the why or how, you now have a problem on your hands. This happens to everyone at least once.

What do you do? [If you didn't go through the ideal client exercises earlier in this chapter, that's the problem!

Back-up, and do the exercises to prevent this from happening again.]

If you find yourself with a challenging client on your hands, you have a few options. First, directly address your observations and ask questions instead of making statements. For example, how does the client think the engagement is going? Ask them on a scale of 1 to 10 how committed they are to the coaching process. Share your observations in a non-judgmental and non-critical way using concrete examples. "Gary, I'm noticing you seem distracted when we meet and haven't moved forward with the last three action steps we agreed on... ."

If the client is not adapting well to your coaching style, consider changing your approach to work better with your client's style. For example, if your coaching has a lot of exercises the client isn't completing, suggest they do the exercises with you, or a partner. Oftentimes, people who are highly relational don't enjoy spending time alone working on tasks.

If directly addressing your concerns and modifying your approach to their style doesn't solve the problem, you can explain you are concerned the engagement will not yield a successful outcome and offer to refund the client's money for services not yet delivered.

I once worked with a career transition client who wanted me to tell her what job to pursue next. I explained my approach would be to help her understand her ideal day at work, but not dictate her job choice. She was disappointed in my response, so I refunded half her money. She would have preferred a career directive over a refund, but that isn't the role of a coach. Ultimately, I also failed to set clear expectations at the start. So, in addition to defining your ideal clients, set clear expectations.

We can't overstate that building a solid understanding of yourself and your ideal clients will limit, or eliminate, difficult client scenarios.

Remember to leverage the *Coach Canvas* summary. It is useful for convincing target clients to work with you and to build your brand.

In the next chapter we will focus on building a strong brand.

5

ℂƷ

BUILD YOUR BRAND
Kristin

Every coach has unique experiences, strengths, values, skills, and personality which influence their approach to coaching. You are equally distinct. The more you understand what your distinctions are, the clearer your brand will be. I covered *The Four Pillars of Career Fit*™ in "Chapter 2: You, the Coach" for this reason.

While defining your distinctions to stand out from other coaches is necessary to build a compelling brand, there is one brand reputation which in-demand coaches share:

They want to help.

Coaches need to be heart-based. When you are genuinely interested in serving and helping others, people are much more likely to trust and feel safe with you. They are also more likely to refer more clients to you.

However, a desire to help, alone, is insufficient to build a reputation that leads to a thriving business. The trait of servant leadership is a cost-of-admission trait into coaching. Beyond a desire to help, what are your stand out characteristics?

When we interviewed Kerri Twigg in "Chapter 1: Coach Stories," we also asked Kerri what makes her different as a coach. She explains what is distinct about her style:

"I've always known my information is not what I'm selling. I'm selling my attention. That's what my business is. You get my empathy, and my mind, and my ears, and my heart on you and your situation. And it feels good. That's what I sell, and it has a lot of value, and I know how people feel when they get it. I see what they could be and that's who I'm speaking with. I meet them where they're at, but I see where they could be, and then I walk them through how to get there."

When people are called to coaching, it's quite common they were coaching people before they were coaches. Others approach them for advice and they informally coached them to navigate through a problem or opportunity.

Why do people come to you for advice?

Let's talk more about why people come to Kerri as an example for you to dig deeper into what your unique brand is as a coach.

UNLOCK YOUR BRAND

Your *strengths, values, preferred skills,* and personality-based *interests* from *The Four Pillars of Career Fit*™ are the key to unlock your brand. Refer back to your *Coach Canvas* and, specifically, the "My Unique Contribution" section of the canvas. This statement is the "seed" your brand grows from.

I shared earlier that our strengths explain *how* we work. If you pay close attention to what people say when they write or speak, we tend to communicate through our strengths.

Your strengths, values, preferred skills, and personality-based interests are the key to unlock your brand – through stories.

Part of why Kerri has a powerful and genuine brand is she knows her strengths and applies them mindfully. Her top five CliftonStrength themes are:

Achiever – Works hard and has a great deal of stamina. "Get it done. Check it off my list."

Futuristic – Inspired by the future and what could be. Energizes others with visions of the future.

Strategic – Faced with any given scenario, quickly spots the relevant patterns and issues.

Positivity – Encouraging, upbeat and enthusiastic and gets others excited about what they are going to do. She wants to bring out the best in people.

Empathy – Senses other people's feelings by imagining herself in others' lives or situations.

Let's break down Kerri's quote above to connect her strengths to her words. I believe you will find this exercise insightful, and you can apply it to your own strengths.

"I've always known my information is not what I'm selling. I'm selling my attention. That's what my business is."

Kerri's *Strategic* theme is speaking. She sees the patterns in how she shows up, and how clients respond to her, which provides her with deeper insight about her coaching.

"You get my empathy, and my mind, and my ears, and my heart on you and your situation. And it feels good. That's what I sell and it has a lot of value and I know how people feel when they get it."

Kerri's *Empathy* is speaking with a nod to her *thinking* strengths (*Futuristic* and *Strategic*) when she says you get her mind. *Empathy* guides her to listen and engage her heart.

"I see what they could be and that's who I'm speaking with."

This is Kerri's *Positivity* theme speaking, combined with the *Futuristic* theme. *Positivity* brings out the best in people, yet because she's also *Futuristic*, she has a vision of what that "best" looks like in the future.

"I meet them where they're at, but I see where they could be, and then I walk them through how to get there."

This statement is another expression of Kerri's *Futuristic* strength. People with *Futuristic* energize people with visions of the future and then structure problem solving so each solution supplies a stepping stone toward that future ("…I walk them through how to get there.").

Not only is Kerri clear on who she is as a coach, she is clear about the clients who choose to work with her and why. Kerri attracts creatives who would not be enticed by the executive coach in a blazer with arms crossed and the words, "I get results!" next to their picture.

If you aren't following Kerri on LinkedIn, I recommend starting. She is a giver and a teacher, and you'll learn a lot from her. As an example, I have included a link to Kerri's insightful article, *How to Use Credibility Stories for Career Growth* in the *Appendix* under Chapter 5.

Your strengths, values, preferred skills, and personality-based interests are the key to unlock your brand through stories.

Think about what you're selling and why people should buy from you. You'll have a chance to complete an activity in this chapter to go deeper.

Let's dig into one more example of using your strengths to find the core elements of your brand. The contrast of two coaches with vastly different strengths will illustrate you don't need to mirror other successful coaches. In fact, you'll experience less success if you take that approach.

LORI, THE STUDENT COACH

Lori Knudsen was a pharmaceutical sales rep for many years until she found herself in a job search in 2018. She was my client.

As part of our engagement, Lori completed the YouMap® assessment. She was inspired by insights she gained about herself and felt drawn to similarly help others. Lori went on to launch *Knowbility Consulting* to help high school and college students gain clarity on who they are and what they do best to equip them to make better major and career choices.

Let's break down why Lori is effective at coaching and, specifically, why she's well suited to work with students and parents. Following are Lori's strengths:

Responsibility – Takes psychological ownership of what she says she will do. She is committed to stable values such as honesty and loyalty.

Parents and students alike can be leery to invest in and work with a coach. Lori is effortlessly responsible and accountable, quickly earning and keeping the trust of both the parent and the student. If either the parent or student does not fully trust a coach, the relationship and coaching will be rife with problems, as mentioned in the last chapter.

Restorative – Adept at dealing with problems. She is good at figuring out what is wrong and resolving it.

Student coaching presents unique challenges which often make it more difficult than working with one person. One such challenge comes from differing, and sometimes competing, expectations between parents and the student.

Lori is adept at generating win/win solutions to problems. She is also able to navigate and resolve hiccups in any process while guiding high school students through career selection, college major and school choice (as well as college alternatives), navigating the application process, interviews and a host of other considerations.

Learner – Great desire to learn and wants to continuously improve.

College students can be overwhelmed to discover all there is to know while preparing for the transition from school to the workplace. Lori takes a lot of the work off her client's plate because of her knowledge and expertise. She is a fountain of knowledge because of the researching, reading, and educating she engages in to keep up with continual changes in processes and requirements. She continually expands her toolkit of resources to equip her clients.

Arranger – Organizes, yet also has a flexibility that complements this ability. She likes to figure out how all the pieces and resources can be arranged for maximum productivity.

Student coaching is about planning for the future and laying out the steps to get to the desired end result. A flexible arranger who sees all the pieces and how they need to fit together is absolutely essential for student coaching. Missed steps or considerations have real world consequences.

Harmony – Natural facilitator that finds consensus. She doesn't enjoy conflict; rather, she seeks areas of agreement.

Recall I mentioned the unique challenges of working with parents and their children, particularly when their expectations are not aligned. Who better than a natural consensus-builder to guide parents and students to align expectations and get on the same page?

Parents and students who lack experience navigating a major life transition together will come to rely heavily on Lori's expertise and planning abilities. Her strong accountability offers relief and the assurance they're well cared for.

I cannot supply the same experience as Lori's. I don't have her same talents that influence her approach with this population. Discovering what you do best that others need most is priceless knowledge and vital for your success. Get clear on what you offer, who would want it, and why they should choose you to provide it.

ACTIVITY:

Reflect on *why* you coach, *benefits* you bring others, and *how coaching benefits you.*

Apply the reflections to answer these questions:

What am I selling?
Who wants to buy it?
Why would they buy it from me?

_____

_____

_____

_____

_____

_____

_____

_____

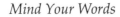 *Mind Your Words*

Look for patterns in the words you write and speak by reviewing content you've written such as client emails, social media posts, resources you have created, copy on your website, or messaging in your LinkedIn summary. Take note of your word choices. What themes come up again and again?

In our interview with Kerri Twigg, we asked her why she believes many coaches struggle to differentiate themselves from other coaches and she shared the following thoughts:

> "It feels like they [coaches] are grasping for something. If you're not consistent and you're always switching [your focus], and not telling us why you're switching, we just think you're jumping from one thing to another. There's no wisdom or depth there. What's their specialty going to be next week? You don't know.

> "Or they're copying what other people are doing and what they think is successful, so they all sound the same. Most of the people who want to be coached want to learn how to have their own voice and how to be themselves. If they can't tell your coaching style from another coach's, then they know you don't have the skill, even if you are saying you have the skill.

> "Potential clients can't tell by the words you're using, or the system you're using, what makes you different from any other coach."

Building your brand is about standing out. Once you know your differentiators, you must explain your competitive advantage in your messaging. We'll expand on the branding work in "Chapter 9: Messaging & Marketing." We have a few topics to cover first.

Let's move on to certifications.

6

⟶ ℭℨ ⟶

COACH CERTIFICATIONS
Kristin & Judi

One question we're often asked is, "Do I need a coaching certification?" The answer to this question is, "It depends." The topic is not cut and dry. Similar to all opinions, different people will tell you different things. We will share conclusions we've reached based on our experiences as coaches in addition to coaching hundreds of other coaches. We also will ask you some questions to help you form your own opinion.

Certain kinds of consulting companies might require specialized business licenses or permits. For example, consultants working on state or federal government projects often require extra permits before bidding on contracts. Consultants working in particular fields, including engineering and health care management, might require industry certification before qualifying for a business license. Because of changing requirements, fees, and industry differences, research to find out what licenses, permits, or certifications, if any, are needed for the coaching or consulting you want to do. Speak to practitioners in the same field or industry to see what insights they can offer.

Outside of specialized circumstances, individual clients rarely care about certifications. In fact, your prospective clients haven't heard of the most well-known certifications in your industry.

When someone is trying to lose weight or get fit, a person identifies someone they know who lost weight and asks that person what they did to get in shape. He or she does not usually try to find a person with a specific fitness credential.

To illustrate this point, following are the top five personal trainer certifications at the time of this writing according to fitnesstrainer.com:

International Sports Sciences Association (ISSA)
The National Council on Strength & Fitness (NCSF)
Fitness Mentors – Personal Training and Online Personal Training Certifications
American Council on Exercise (ACE)
National Academy of Sports Medicine (NASM)

Kristin:

Despite being an avid runner and deeply into personal fitness, I could not name any of the five fitness credentials prior to looking them up. In February 2021, I joined an online running group led by a woman, Carey Adam, who went to high school with my exercise partner. I had no idea what certifications the woman had. I knew my partner trusted her and achieved results by taking part in her programs. My partner's results were all I needed to know.

After six months, my expectations were exceeded and I renew the membership annually. I'm reaching results beyond what I thought possible, yet I still could not tell you which certifications Carey holds.

In my prior years of coaching and speaking to thousands of prospective clients, I had exactly one person ask about my certifications. Not only did the prospect not ask for specifics, but they merely inquired, "You have a coaching certification, right?" After responding in the affirmative, the prospective client shifted the conversation to another topic.

One exception to certification disinterest is when working with corporate clients who require you to send Requests for Proposals (RFPs) to secure a contract. While RFPs vary, the form you must complete will contain questions about your credentials.

I have two main objections with some certifications. My first objection is when the certification supplies little to no coaching knowledge, nor a method or framework. The certification's purpose is merely to place a stamp of approval on your existing coaching. Ideally, your clients place the stamp of approval on your coaching through their referrals and testimonials.

My second concern is when certifying organizations require annual or bi-annual recertification. Recertifications feel a bit like a racket whose main function is to generate added revenue for the certifying body. There are exceptions of course, and that is when a certification has technology or knowledge with a short shelf-life, and you would be supplying inaccurate and even dangerous advice if you did not obtain recertification.

I don't object to all certifications. In fact, many of them are quite useful. One example is obtaining a certification to use a specific tool or assessment. Every certification I've obtained was to help me coach using a specific tool. A certification of this nature can ensure you administer and debrief an assessment as intended by the publisher. Assessments are meant to be instructive, not conclusive, and the publisher should also supply ethical guidelines for use.

I will leave you with a few questions to consider:

Do you lack a reliable and repeatable coaching process?
Do you feel your process has gaps you should fill?
Do you lack confidence with your current process?
Are you inconsistent in getting strong client results?

If you answered "yes" to any of these questions, maybe the right certification could help close these gaps. If you answered "no," perhaps a certification isn't needed right now. Next, Judi will share her experience.

Judi:

I discovered the world of psychometric tools when I went for career coaching in my early thirties. I was hooked at once.

Over eight weeks working with a skilled facilitator, I took a number of assessments that helped me learn a tremendous amount about myself. But I had a GED, not even a high school diploma, so I knew I would need to learn from a skilled professional if I was ever going to use these tools. And that's what I did. I also enrolled in university and over eight years earned a bachelor's degree.

When I decided to leave the corporate world, my first step was deciding which tools would give me the expertise and credibility I knew I needed. Then I paid for certification in those tools. Back then, certification involved pre-work, travelling to a location for training, meals, hotels, etc. But I knew having the qualifications would boost my self-confidence, so I went for it.

Similarly, most of the coaches and consultants I knew had graduate degrees, so I decided I would go to graduate school, and I'm really glad I did. Finally, I had heard it was possible to get certified as a consultant, and so I went that route as well.

Bottom line, I have never wanted anyone to say to me, "We'd love to have you do this work but you lack (fill in the blank – degree, certification, experience, etc.)," so I did all three. I initially did not get a coaching certification. I am very practical, so I started talking to people I knew who had a reputation as an excellent coach. I asked them about their coaching practice and their experience. I also joined a master mind of coaches. Those two things have served me well. Because of my extensive experience and my clients all being repeats or referrals, I am never asked if I'm certified as a coach.

After a decade of coaching, I went through a process to gain certification in business coaching and executive coaching. Because of my experience, I was simply allowed to take the exams which I passed. Here are some questions to ask yourself to help decide about certification.

Will this increase my confidence?

Will it give me real tools I can use?

Does it make sense to me?

Can I see how it will quickly develop my skills?

Bottom line – preparation is everything. I wanted to be sure I felt totally prepared, so I pursued certification (at least for assessments), education (my M.S. in Organizational Development) and practical learning from outstanding coaches. This path is not for everyone. There are many ways to prepare. Learning from other coaches is one of the most important.

We've covered a lot of ground focusing on you, the coach or consultant. It's time to shift focus to starting your business.

7

—————— ℭℨ ——————

STARTING A BUSINESS
Kristin

SHOULD I START MY OWN BUSINESS?

How do you know if you're cut out to be a business owner or entrepreneur? Are successful self-employed people hard-wired to be successful business owners, or can it be learned?

Gary Vaynerchuk, CEO of VaynerMedia, believes the top entrepreneurs who pull in $500,000+ in annual revenue do have a hard-wired talent. However, he also believes you can become the best version of yourself as an entrepreneur by studying, putting yourself out there, and by learning your craft.

Vaynerchuk references the example of athletics. When people think of athletes, their mind goes to the highest level of playing in the National Hockey League, National Football League, National Basketball Association, or Major League Baseball. Even though the ultimate measure of success for playing sports appears to be making it to the big leagues, many athletes have found success in smaller arenas. The same can apply to one's thinking when starting a coaching business. You don't need to reach the top one percent of coaches to be, or feel, successful.

If you can start a business that allows you to enjoy your work, live life on your terms, and earn a comfortable living, not fretting about money, doesn't that also sound like success?

Coach practitioners, excluding athletic and sports coaches, reported an average annual income from coaching of about $61,900, which is higher than the annual median salary of all U.S. workers.[7]

One factor that will decide if you can make it as a coach is steeling yourself to other people's opinions. People will criticize you, question you, and offer a variety of unsolicited advice when you go down a path of self-employment. Usually there are two motivations for what feels like opposition leveled against your goals:

1. They are envious of you for boldly following your ambitions.

2. They care about you and are scared for you. Listen, anyone who is scared by what you're doing is not wired for success in what you're trying to do. Also, coaching and entrepreneurship is different from a regular job, making it harder for others to relate.

In both cases, you must learn to push through opposition and believe in yourself, even if you're the only one who does. When we believe in ourselves, we create opportunity instead of waiting for opportunities, and we project a confidence (not arrogance) that others are attracted to.

If you're currently working for a company and want to become your own boss, consider if coaching within your organization before stepping out on your own is a strategy that could work for you. You can build your experience and amass coaching success stories, refine and sharpen your coaching process, and build your coaching confidence on someone else's dime without having to hustle for clients.

If you're currently coaching in an organization and want to start a side hustle, or you already have a side hustle and want to transition into working for yourself full-time, your employer could become your first big client.

A.K. is a leader in her organization and has a coaching practice on the side. To fulfill her goal of coaching more in her day job, she decided to submit a proposal to create a role in Human Resources as a YouMap® Coach.

I had a call with A.K. to discuss her approach in creating a pitch to present this idea to Human Resources. She planned to outline and present a case for how her proposed coaching program would help the organization and align to the company's goals. Following are the elements A.K. included in her thorough proposal:

Overview - Highlights of industry trends such as the Great Resignation and the need to improve talent acquisition and talent management. She addressed how the proposed role could improve retention rates, job satisfaction, and the company's reputation as an employer of choice.

Objective - A.K. connected some of the stated goals of the organization to her proposed initiative. She selected three specific goals of the organization to highlight.

Opportunity – A.K. chose to highlight five specific opportunities her proposal would create and how they would help the organization:

1. As employees understand who they are – strengths, values, skills, and personality – they are more empowered to bring their authentic selves to work and to seek the right position to take best advantage of what makes them unique.

2. When employees can share with their manager who they are via a career profile, managers can right-fit employees in existing roles while helping their employees to design their future career paths.

3. When employers invest in employees' career journeys, the employees in turn feel more invested in the company and experience greater job satisfaction.

4. By right-fitting employees to roles – either via role modification or career mobility – employee job satisfaction and retention is increased.

5. When employers partner with low-performing employees to find the reasons for poor role fit, even employees who exit have a more positive

impression of the company, as reflected via positive exit postings on career boards such as GlassDoor or Indeed.

Solution – The outline of her proposed pilot program included who would be targeted, the suggested pilot duration, coaching methods to be used and delivery modalities such as 1:1 coaching and workshops. She also proposed that 25 percent of her time be dedicated to the pilot and 75 percent of her time dedicated to her full-time position to reduce the risk of the pilot program.

Proposal – The outline of the pilot also included how the pilot would work, the rationale, execution plan, resources to be provided by the coach and the company, timeline of execution, pricing, and expected results of the pilot program.

A.K. concluded her proposal with suggested next steps should the pilot prove successful, such as continuing the program beyond the pilot, developing the pilot into a full-time position, and expanding the program to other regions by certifying more coaches in the organization.

I proposed something similar when I started my business as a side hustle. My employer became my first corporate client. I had been on a small team of people who launched a high potential leadership development program at the company. My responsibility within the program included the mentoring part, which involved coaching each participant for ten months, once monthly, throughout the program.

Later, upon giving my resignation from the organization, I pitched a proposal to continue supporting the leadership development program as a contractor. I had held positions both as an Operations Manager and Senior Operations Manager in the company. All the participants in the program were being groomed for leadership in those positions, which was a unique advantage I brought to the table.

I also had certifications and coaching experience in the assessments that would be used in the curriculum. This unique skill stack positioned me as a top choice to continue coaching these individuals and influenced the decision maker to accept my proposal.

The concept of a skill stack has been around a while, but many are still unfamiliar with the term. The idea is that instead of thinking of the skills you've gained as separate and unrelated from one another, you should try to wed a few related skills that might not seem related. Your skills can be spun together into a wider skill set that makes you uniquely and distinctly talented at your profession.

American writer, John Grisham, is an excellent example of using your unique skill stack. He joins J.K. Rowling and Tom Clancy as the only authors in history to sell 200 million copies on a first printing. With the success of his second novel, *The Firm*, Grisham quit practicing law to write full-time. In his youth, Grisham had no interest in writing. A case inspired him to write his first novel, *A Time to Kill*, which was rejected by 28 publishers before being accepted by an unknown publishing house.

Grisham wove his *experience* with law into his writing instead of leaving law entirely behind. He also likely brought *transferrable skills* from criminal law and litigation to his writing. Following are some of the skills that transfer between the two professions:

- Analytical and research skills
- Attention to detail
- Organizational skills
- Time management
- Persuasive communication
- Written communication skills
- Interpersonal skills

What is the skill stack you're uniquely positioned to offer that will help your prospective clients?

You have unique offerings you may not have considered. The self-discovery exercises found throughout chapters two through four will help with this, in particular the "Strengths," "Skills," and "The 3 C's of Coaching" exercises in Chapter 2. We will also dig deeper into finding a niche in "Chapter 13: Niches."

The acceptance of my proposal by my former employer led to three consecutive one-year contracts that supplied the seed revenue to grow my business. During those three years, I developed some passive income strategies and focused on growing my business so I would not be dependent on the revenue long term. Having one large client is a significant risk to your business.

CHICKENS AND PIGS IN BUSINESS

Harold Star's book *Chicken and Pigs – Business Models and Competitive Strategies* puts businesses into four categories. Star's model is based on customer transaction frequency (how often they buy from you) and revenue contribution from each transaction.

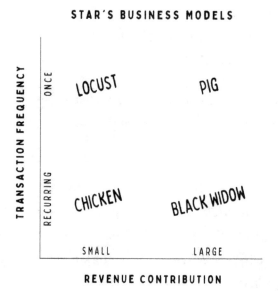

Let's review each of the four business models, and how this relates to your coaching or consulting practice, or other service business.

Locust Business

A Locust business is built on large numbers of one-time transactions at low revenue per transaction. Profit margins are slim and rely on high traffic sales. Walmart, Amazon, and grocery stores are examples of the Locust business model.

For a coaching or consulting practice, this is not an ideal business model as it requires constant refilling of the customer pipeline with low revenue per client.

Chicken Business

Similar to the Locust business model, a Chicken business also yields low revenue per transaction. However, Chicken businesses deliver a more substantial revenue impact because transactions are recurring (think laying lots of eggs). While Amazon started out as Locust business, they have since expanded into cloud computing services, which is a subscription model that makes them even more successful as a Chicken business.

In a Chicken business, customers take part in regular, recurring transactions. Examples of recurring transactions are memberships and subscriptions like streaming music services or auto-deliveries of online nutrition supplements.

Do you have an automated service or product such as recorded webinars, workshops, or training you could offer through a membership or subscription?

PIG BUSINESS

A Pig business depends on high dollar one-time projects, like consulting and coaching. You work with a variety of clients at premium rates. People are more willing to pay for a specific expertise or product they can't easily find elsewhere, but the projects may be fewer and far between.

If you can become a highly regarded coach, you are a Pig business. People with big and important projects will come to you, even though there may be others who can do what you do.

Executive coaches as a rule use the Pig business format. They are chosen for a project and are not asked to bid. When you become a trusted resource for a large endeavor (businesses with annual revenue or budgets in excess of a billion dollars), the work renews effortlessly because they don't want to start over with someone new.

Clients see you as someone who is competent and they like working with you. Be careful not to over-rely on one client. You don't want to become a Black Widow business.

BLACK WIDOW BUSINESS

A Black Widow business is highly dependent on a small number of customers for its revenue. For example, a consulting firm dedicated to one large corporate client, a vendor dedicated to working with a national box store, or a Federal government contract.

The business recurs because the client is large, but if your entire business is based on a Black Widow model, you could be on shaky ground. When that client ends your relationship, or goes out of business, your revenue stream instantly dries up.

Star's book is titled *Chicken and Pigs* because the combination or blend of the Chicken and Pig models offer an ideal setup to successfully grow and scale a business.

I was exposed to the Chicken and Pig business model before starting my coaching and consulting business, which led me to adopt this approach with my practice.

My Pig business is a coaching certification program. At the time of this writing, I offer only four or five trainings per year and enroll a small number of participants in each cohort. I also have a small number of certified Master Trainers, people who can also certify coaches, consultants, and leaders.

Becoming certified as a YouMap® coach is not something that can be obtained elsewhere, making the credential more exclusive. Spend time thinking about your signature offering or other distinctives not easily found among other coaches.

My Chicken business is an online store on my website where individuals can buy various YouMap® products, from books to assessments to uncover strengths, values, preferred skills and personality-based interests in children, teens, and adults. While many of the purchases are one-time, we often have coaches, recruiters, and team leaders who are repeat buyers for their employees or clients. I also have a small segment of my business based on the Locust model – career books for adults and self-discovery books for children.

Recall I mentioned my former employer offered me a contract to coach within their high potential leadership program. Yes, my brand-new business was a classic Black Widow model. I'm not recommending that you completely reject a Black Widow business opportunity. Black Widow contracts can be lucrative yet volatile. They carry significant risk and place you in a vulnerable position, so you don't want to camp there.

When I entered into a Black Widow business model, I quickly began the process of diversifying my company by creating a Chicken business to financially sustain my business between Pig projects.

IS THE HUSTLE & GRIND NECESSARY TO SUCCEED?

The hustle and grind culture is popular fodder for influencer posts on social media. Yet only you can define what success will look like for you. Success is very personal and individualized.

Hustling and grinding for the sake of it doesn't make a lot of sense. Your business should align to your values, and you should reflect on what you want to get out of having your own business. This activity will help you define your vision of your business.

ACTIVITY:

Imagine you have an ideal business.

List the elements or characteristics that illustrate what your successful practice should look like.

How does each characteristic reveal values that matter to you?

Here is an example to help you with this activity:

My ideal practice will:

- Focus on the talents/skills I enjoy and avoid activities that burn me out. *Autonomy is important to me. I want to dictate how I spend my work day.*

- Serve self-motivated clients who desire to improve. *I like working with others who value excellence. I will be frustrated by clients who aren't committed to being their best.*

- Be based on 80 percent referrals and 20 percent business development. *Selling drains me. A client ambassador model will help reduce selling.*

- Give me the flexibility to set my schedule and pursue other interests and hobbies. *I need balance to spend time with family, to exercise, and travel.*

- Generate enough revenue to cover expenses, take a trip each year, and have an emergency fund of six months of expenses. *I am not driven by money but must feel stable and want to be able to travel.*

My ideal practice will:

_____

_____

_____

_____

_____

_____

_____

_____

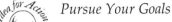 *Pursue Your Goals*

Once you have worked out the details of your successful practice, you will need to create practical, actionable goals to usher your desired business into reality.

What questions will you ask yourself based on the characteristics you outlined in your desired practice? These questions will enable you to create the right goals.

For example, following are questions based on the example from the last activity:

What services will use my talents and skills?

What is my ideal client and how will I create messaging to attract these people?

How do I create ambassadors?

How many hours per week do I plan to work in the early days of my business and as time goes on? What will my schedule look like?

How much revenue do I need to earn in the first, second, and third year of my business?

How many clients do I need to secure, and how much do I need to charge to meet my annual revenue goals?

Some of these questions have been addressed and others will be answered as you read further in this book.

Now, back to the question, "Is the hustle and grind necessary?" Usually, at first, but not forever.

Personal finance personality, radio show host, author, and businessperson Dave Ramsey once said on his show that when you start a sales job, the way to get ahead so you're not in a constant grind is to do two years' worth of work in the first two months. When you are a coach or consultant, you are in sales, too.

How can you work two years in two months? Well, research suggests we aren't productive every hour of the workday, so you're not cramming a bunch of eight-hour days into that time period. In an eight-hour day, the average worker is only productive for two hours and 53 minutes. When you work within your strengths and interests, your productivity increases 600 percent, according to Gallup.

Another factor is committing to remain fiercely focused on where you spend your time, cutting time wasters and interruptions. We'll expand on this in "Chapter 24: Time Management" in the "Coach!" section.

Ramsey's approach is exactly what I did when I started my business. In 2014, I took on my first client when a co-worker asked me to coach her husband. I decided to make my business official by registering the business with the state of North Carolina, then opened a bank account as a sole proprietor. Seven months later, on June 12, 2015, I left my job to work for myself. I still remember that sweet day!

In the beginning, I worked a lot of hours building, speaking, writing, creating, and coaching. I realized quickly that working 100 hours every week was going to eventually burn me out. In 2016, I started writing books so I could secure more speaking engagements. Beginning in 2018, I focused heavily on building passive income so I could generate revenue while I slept without my presence needed.

Less than two years later, this strategic investment allowed me to pivot from coaching individuals to focus on writing full time, certifying coaches, and innovating my product. I went from conducting six to eight coaching meetings per day, to having two or three meetings per week. In addition, I only spend 40 hours per year certifying coaches.

I begin my workday at 11:00 a.m. and finish at 3:00 p.m. I run or lift weights in the morning and stop working when I pick my kids up from school. Yes, I did grind, but it was just a few years. If you don't want to grind into the sunset, you can set your business up in a way that you don't have to, such as passive income and building a referral-based business. We'll talk about all this, and more, throughout the book.

Now, let's review some commonly asked questions about side hustles.

SIDE HUSTLE FAQS

Can I start a business while working for my employer?

Proactively speak to your Human Resources department about your intention to start a business on the side. They will be able to speak to the company's "moonlighting" policy. Some companies simply require you to disclose a side business, others allow side businesses as long as your services are not competitive with the company and the work is not done on company time.

Should I create a sole proprietorship (DBA) or an LLC?

Melinda Emerson, The Small Biz Lady, recommends incorporating your business as an LLC or S-Corp. For your first business with only you as an employee, an LLC is sufficient. Starting your business as a sole proprietor uses your personal social security number. You are at risk for personal legal liability with this business arrangement. An LLC also appears more professional, particularly for executive and corporate clients.

You can hire a small business or entrepreneurial attorney to help set up your business. However, there is no legal requirement to use an attorney. Services like LegalZoom are simple and affordable to set up an LLC. Conduct research to choose the most desirable choice.

Carrie, an entrepreneur friend, told me she invested $10,000 to start up her business. She has contracts, agreements, various forms, terms and conditions and a privacy policy for her website. Her attorney created documents she hadn't even thought of needing. Everything was taken care of. Not everyone can make this investment, but at least check in with an attorney.

She suggests you might even find one at a local networking event; they're always there!

Note that LegalZoom cannot supply legal advice. The service manages the process, including completing required forms and documentation for you to sign, then sending the documentation on your behalf.

I used LegalZoom to start my first business because of an allergy to filling out documentation. If you also are allergic to administration, Melinda Emerson has a blog and podcast to make starting a business less overwhelming.

What steps should I take to start my business?

First things first, you must register your business name with your state, and then open a business bank account, in that order. You cannot open a bank account without first registering a business. There is a small cost associated to do so.

Research your business name to ensure it is available prior to registering. You can do a search on where to register a business for your geographic location.

Every state has a Secretary of State or other agency responsible for business entity filings. In most states, the website of the state business filing agency includes an online entity name check tool. You can use the online tool to search business names and find out whether another business is already using the name you have chosen.

You should also consider consulting with a small business attorney so you are aware of your options.

The US Small Business Administration (SBA) has published a free guide called *10 Steps to Start Your Small Business*.[2] You can find a link to the guide in the *Appendix*.

How much will it cost to start a side hustle?

To estimate your startup costs, there are three things you need to consider:

1. Expenses you'll incur before you start. For example, legal expenses, marketing expenses, subscriptions, technology, certifications, etc.

2. Assets other than cash you'll need to supply the business before you start, such as inventory.

3. Money you need to have in the business bank account to fund expenses during the early stage of the business when sales aren't likely to cover costs and expenses.

The Small Business Administration offers a free *Calculate Your Startup Costs* guide.[3] You can find a link to the guide in the *Appendix*.

What is a business plan? Do I need one?

A business plan serves as a roadmap for your business. It includes things like the problems your business will solve, your competitive advantages, the structure and services or products of your business, how you plan to attract customers, funding requirements, and financial projections.

You don't need to create an exhaustive business plan if you are a solopreneur, but it's a good exercise to think through the elements of a basic business plan and get things out of your head and on paper. The SBA offers a free guide to help you write a business plan.[4] You can find a link to the guide in the *Appendix*. Review and update your business plan at least once yearly, which most successful businesses do.

The US Small Business Administration offers a free 10-step guide to start your business, a guide to calculate start-up costs, and a how-to guide for writing a business plan. NerdWallet also offers a lot of business and financial resources, including how to calculate startup costs. Access the links to these resources in the Appendix.

How do I brand my LinkedIn profile and other social media when I have a job and a side hustle?

Brand your profile to align with where you are headed. Attempting to communicate two distinct brands on social media will create confusion.

How will I know when it's time to leave my employer and work for myself full-time?

How many hours are you willing to work? Do you have a family? Do you have support to help with kids if you are a parent?

When I started my side hustle, I chose Monday through Thursday evenings to do coaching, reserving weekends for personal and family time. I was not willing to let my side business sprawl into my weekend on a regular basis.

Once I was putting in about 20-25 hours each week in my side hustle, on top of the hours in my day job, I decided to quit. This is truly a personal decision. You can base your decision on how many hours you're working each week or by how often new clients are coming in the door.

For example, if you are landing a new client every week, quitting your job to focus on your side hustle is a good bet. If you are still seeing a month go by without a new client, it's premature to quit *unless* you've saved an expense fund that enables you to quit your job.

Another consideration is the reason you are staying in your job. If your day job is affecting your health, sometimes you can't stay where you are, even if it makes financial sense. I have a friend who was working for a manager that created a toxic environment. Her hair began falling out from stress.

Sometimes people stay because they can't give up the security. In reality, a company can let you go (at least in the United States) whenever they want. Security is an illusion.

I'm certain you have many more questions. Take time to create and reflect on your *Coach Canvas* from "Part I: Ready." The first part of the book focused on you—from discovering who you are as a coach or consultant, to getting clear on the clients you want to serve, the decision to obtain certifications, the kind of brand you want to create, and the various decisions you must make when starting a business.

Talk to other coaches and benefit from their experience. When I started my coaching business, my mother saved me a lot of headaches by sharing her knowledge, insights, tips and tricks, since she started a coaching practice 20 years before I started mine.

The next chapter goes into more detail on the financial considerations you need to think about when starting a coaching or consulting business.

8

❧

FINANCIAL CONSIDERATIONS
Kristin

If you are considering leaving a position of employment to work for yourself, it's considered best practice to save three months of expenses if you have a dual income household and six months of expenses if you have a single income household.

A good first step to start a business is to create a dedicated savings fund. Start small, estimate your expected costs, and conservatively project your cash flow, which is the total amount of cash flowing in and out of your business. If you are not reading the book in order, "Chapter 7: Starting a Business" shares more details for starting up a business.

If you're starting a business, or have started one, be cautious not to scale up too early without the cash to back it up. When I initially started my business, I wanted to build an automated software solution to send YouMap® assessments and generate reports rather than employing a manual process. The estimated cost of the online system would be approximately $500,000 and would take one software developer a year to build.

My husband works in software consulting services and convinced me my plan wasn't solid. The mantra "If we build it, they will come," can put entrepreneurs out of business. At first I disagreed but decided to follow his advice. He was right. By waiting until my business had a steady flow of customers, client revenue funded my business expansion instead of bootstrapping my business from personal funds. The bottom line is to keep your overhead as low as possible and prioritize mission-critical investments.

Crowdfunding is a possibility through Kickstarter or GoFundMe. Campaigns with videos including your purpose will do better than without a video because people will better connect with your story. Keep the campaign to a month. Longer campaigns don't do as well.

Networking with angel investors is another possibility for startups. A solopreneur coach is less likely to go this route, but if you have a proprietary product, investors are more likely to hear you out. Make sure you have a compelling "why" to help people connect with your mission and vision. Below are eight places to find angel investors:

- AngelList, a website to seek investors for funding
- Angel Capital Association
- Gust
- Angel Forum
- Angel Investment Network
- Social Media
- Networking Events
- Friends and Family

Setting revenue goals will help you make business decisions. Let's say your annual earning target is $50,000 in your first full year of business, $60,000 your second year, $75,000 in year three, and $100,000 by year five.

Your revenue goal will help you decide what to charge and how many clients you must secure to reach your target. For example, if your revenue goal is $50,000 and your mid-priced service package is $1,499, you will need to land thirty-four clients to reach your revenue goal. In other words, you should be prepared to gain three paying clients each month during the year. You can adjust pricing as needed based on a reasonable estimate of clients you are able to bring in. You don't want to set your rates so high that you aren't competitive. Nor do you want to undersell yourself by setting your rates too low. See "Chapter 11: Proposals" and "Chapter 12: Services & Pricing" for more guidance.

As a rule of thumb, if you are the primary wage earner and have serious life expenses ahead of you (e.g. college tuition for children), plan to buy a house, or have existing debt, you need to earn in excess of $150,000 in coaching within the first two to three years. If you aren't able to do this, then coaching will have to be something you enjoy on the side, not the primary source of your income. Again, this is just a rule of thumb. If you go through the steps to understand your financial picture and household expenses, you will be better prepared to set targeted revenue goals for your business.

According to Forbes, most businesses are not profitable in their first year.[5] Of the businesses that become profitable, it is estimated it takes two to three years to reach profitability.[6] Amazon's first profitable year was recorded ten years after its founding.

Judi: A note to women. Angelique Rewers, Founder of The Corporate Agent, says only about two percent of female coaches earn six figures annually. I speculate this is because there is a mismatch on "The 3 C's of Coaching" we shared earlier (Coach what you know, Combine what you know with your abilities, and Care deeply about the work). If any of these three principles are missing in your practice, your credibility is at risk.

If you aspire to be a business or corporate coach, Angelique is a gold mine of ideas to help you generate revenue on either side of the actual delivery of the service. Google and follow her.

Other key factors to consider are your expenses and taxes.

EXPENSES

As mentioned previously, keep costs low. Use contractors and freelancers for services you need rather than hiring employees until you have more consistent sales coming in. This includes an assistant. You can pay virtual assistants by the hour instead of placing them on your payroll. An assistant, even if only a few hours a week, is a wise expense.

Let's say you charge a set rate for one-hour strategy sessions with clients. Every time you spend one hour on administrative activities, that is time you are not generating revenue. Your time is best spent doing paid work, on activities that grow your business within your zone of expertise.

Instead, invest in a virtual assistant (VA) for administrative tasks. To start, budget a few hours per week for a VA when planning your business expenses. Many VAs work for multiple solopreneurs so it is fine if you only have four weekly hours of work available. A small weekly investment frees up to time to engage in high value activities that will actually grow your business. Employing a VA also projects a more successful business image than prospective clients seeing you juggling your own administrative tasks.

Spend money on what you *actually* need instead of what you *think* a business needs. You need a way to invoice people and receive their money. Fancy technology that isn't your core product, employees, social media ads, business cards, and office space are often unnecessary expenses for a brand-new coach or consultant. It's a solid idea to fund enhancements with client revenue, unless you've budgeted and saved money in advance.

When I first started my business, I didn't immediately use a scheduling tool. I also didn't have a website on day one. I initially used my LinkedIn profile as my point of contact because that is where most prospective clients found me. Once I had more than one client at a time, I bought an annual subscription for a scheduling tool and invested in a simple website.

Talk to people you know who own a business about the mistakes they made and learn from those mistakes instead of making them. You might consider joining a couple of coach groups or forums to see what other coaches are discussing and ask your own questions.

TAXES

Ah, taxes. The small business owner's least favorite word. When you are an employee, your taxes are automatically taken out of your paycheck. Not so when you work for yourself. At tax time you will be in for a rude awakening if you haven't set aside money to pay your taxes. Even if you reinvest your revenue back into your business, that income is taxable.

At the time of this writing, you must file a US income tax return if your business earns $400 or more. Each quarter, set aside at least 30 percent of what you earn to cover your state and federal taxes. You will also need to track all revenue and expenses as small businesses are an often-targeted group for audits.

Talk to an accountant, preferably one who has been referred to you by a satisfied business owner, to receive more detailed tax guidance based on where you live.

SPEND MONEY TO MAKE MONEY

It is often said you have to spend money to make money. Not all expenditures are equal. Some wise investments for your business include:

- Contracted administrative assistant a few hours per week. Free yourself up to work on your business and serve your clients. You will grow faster if you aren't bogged down with administration.
- Reputable bookkeeping services.
- Billing and payment processing services such as PayPal, Stripe, Square, Due, etc. Being able to professionally invoice and receive payment is a crucial business process.
- Reinvesting money back into the business. Having a cushion in your business bank account can help you keep your doors open if you encounter an unexpected expense.

We've reached the end of the "Ready" section of the book! Revisit this section throughout your career and update your *Coach Canvas* periodically, such as after major career or life changes. Our values and skills change, and so does our motivation.

In "Part II: Set," we will help you set your business and processes up for success so you can focus on coaching, which we cover in the third and final section of the book.

PART II: SET

Hang up your shingle and clients will come, right? Not quite.

Once you know the kind of coach you are and who you help, you must ensure your business can run smoothly. This section, "Set," helps you set your business up for success.

Many tasks will compete for your time. We've focused this section on the most important priorities.

Consider the following questions:

How do I market my services?

Do I need to use contracts?

How do I create a proposal?

What if a client backs out or doesn't pay an invoice?

Do I need to have a niche?

How can I generate leads?

How can I attract clients if selling is uncomfortable for me?

How do I deal with requests to work for free?

How do I stop giving everything away?

How do I hire an assistant? I'm not sure I can afford one.

In this section of the book, we'll address the above questions, and more. Let's start with messaging and marketing.

9

───────── ⚈ ─────────

MESSAGING & MARKETING

Kristin

A common challenge for coaches and consultants is creating compelling messaging which piques the interest of prospective clients. Coaching and consulting jargon embedded in your messaging does not usually connect with potential customers.

Deliver your message in the language of your client.

Rather than speaking like a coach, speak like someone who gets it because you've been there, too. You want your clients to see themselves in what you share. This is why knowing who you want to help, and why, is so important. Show your client your empathy for their situation by using the language your clients actually use.

Following is an example of jargon-filled messaging:

I help you navigate your journey to
live with Passion, Power, and Purpose.

Is it clear what the outcome of working with this coach will be? How do you know your definition of passion, power, and purpose are the same as the coach?

During discovery calls with your clients, what do they say they need help with? Living with passion, power, and purpose is not what clients are saying to the coach. While passion, power, and purpose might be what a client wants, this messaging is not straightforward to most people. Power can mean many different things, for example. Does power mean boldness, power associated with status and authority, both or something else?

Messaging should be clear, concise, and leave prospective clients with a keen sense of the results you guide them toward. Be distinct about the outcomes you deliver. Where do you find this language? Simply from the people who talk to you.

Idea for Action *Capture the Voice of Your Ideal Customer*

When speaking to anyone and everyone about the work you do, pay attention to the words people choose when discussing and describing situations where you can help.

For years, I kept documents where I would summarize what prospective clients told me. I noted the words and phrases that surfaced repeatedly when I networked, spoke to friends or family, or chatted with a stranger on a plane about their careers.

Here are example phrases I repeatedly heard:

I want to be in an environment where I can be appreciated.

I struggle to find a career that is challenging and fulfilling.

I'm drained at the end of every day.

I want to be myself at work.

Identify the common phrases you hear that connect to what you do best and turn them into questions:

Are you feeling unappreciated at work?

Do you struggle to find a challenging and rewarding career?

Do you feel drained at the end of most work days?

Do you feel you can't be yourself at work?

Questions place your audience into the experiences they've had related to the question you have posed. Reliving the experience creates an emotional reaction. This gives you the opportunity to paint the opposite picture using powerful words such as *imagine*. Finally, share customer testimonials that relate to the imagined and desired future state of your prospect.

Strong messaging hinges on interesting storytelling. Stories are important because they are a fundamental part of being human. Before the written word, storytelling was the only method our ancestors had to pass on traditions and knowledge.

Judi: You must tell stories people can relate to that have a universal truth embedded. People love fairy tales and to be read to as children. Why? Because those stories all have the kernel of a universal truth — something we can all identify with and take something from. Stories make us feel like we aren't alone. Everybody loves stories, even when they say they don't!

The stories you tell prospective clients have three important functions:

1. Encourage the listener.
2. Remind the listener he or she is not alone.
3. Move the listener to action.

I mentioned using the language of your customers in your stories above. If you're new to coaching and lack "voice of the customer" data, social media is a great place to get content for stories.

Create a post on a platform where you are likely to get the most engagement. Begin your post with a hook, such as a rhetorical question. Next, tell a story or share your knowledge on a topic. Tag people who you know will have something valuable to add. Make it clear you understand the situation because you have experienced it yourself or you've helped someone who did. A story is relatable when people can see themselves in it.

Finally, include a call to action after you tell the story. My favorite method is to ask a question. People *love* to give their opinions. "What would you tell your 18-year-old self" posts often attract a larger number of responses because regret is a universal principle.

You don't need to pose a question that applies to everyone. If you are serving a specific niche, ask questions unique to your client population, situations they all face. For example, job seekers tend to experience frustration, hopelessness, job application fatigue, or feelings of rejection.

Asking job seekers the hardest thing about looking for a job can give you content ideas for weeks.

Collect the responses and save them for your marketing efforts. You can create a lot of content based on answers to your questions. In fact, you can ask questions to give you content ideas for a host of uses. When I wrote this book, I posed a question to my LinkedIn connections asking what I should include in this book. I saved the responses in a file and reviewed them when I started planning the book with my mother.

CREATE YOUR STORIES

In addition to stories for marketing content, you need stories about yourself. Your stories might include the *why* behind the work you do, or why you help the people you do. Other stories might be about your journey, how you ended up where you are today. You can, and should, tell client success stories – anonymously. If you're transitioning into coaching from another field, you need a story that explains that as well.

First, get a package of index cards. Write down one story from your career on a card each day for seven to ten days. Accomplishments from your coaching experience are most relevant. If you haven't formally begun coaching, use transferable examples from your career where you advised, trained, mentored, used your intuition, strategized, or helped someone with a problem.

Some people can take these instructions and run with them; others might need some prompts. Try these ideas:

1. Write down a story about a time you led someone to a breakthrough.
2. What was the biggest impact you've had on a client?
3. What is your favorite client success story?
4. When did you have flow in your work, where time stopped and this flow allowed a wonderful thing to happen?
5. What is the best compliment you've received from someone you helped? Why were you given the compliment?
6. What situation did you face that makes you relatable to your clients and illustrates you understand their situation?
7. What is one of your proudest accomplishments in your career?
8. What stories from your life reveal overcoming adversity, perseverance, resilience, or other universal principles? Everyone loves the hero's journey.
9. When did a door close only to have a better one open?
10. Who are the people who have positively impacted your life, and how did they affect you?

Your stories create opportunities to appear human and relatable to others. Standing on a pedestal doling out expertise without humanizing yourself misses an opportunity to build trust with your audience.

Find Your Voice

Idea for Action

Do you struggle to sound authentic in marketing copy? Do you use stuffy language or jargon that sounds like a "template" of every other coach?

Find your voice by using a voice recording app and pretend you're catching up with an old friend. *Tell them what you do for work, why you love it, and your best story about a person you helped.*

Speak from the soul and listen to the recording. Did you notice when you became animated? Capture words and phrases you spoke. You speak your strengths, values, and motivation. When you write for an audience, the brain monitors, edits, censors and second guesses. When you speak, words flow.

Recently I spoke with a coach who told me, "I believe in humans. If we can dig down deep into what excites us and what could be, we can't fail." Her website starts with, "I help mid-career professionals see their skillset from a different perspective, so they gain the clarity and confidence required for career transition."

What a stark difference in passion! Give it a try.

One final note about finding your voice. Remember to refer to your *Coach Canvas*. In "Chapter 2: You, the Coach," I explained your *personality-based interests* are expressed through your *skills*. Your interests and skills can help you decide what medium to use to market your services, and the focus of your content.

For example, if you are a *thinker* and a *helper*, you can create *thought-provoking* content that *helps* people delivered through your preferred *skills*. Or, if you like *training*, lead a free webinar. If you like *presenting*, create a video or give a talk. If you like *writing*, start a newsletter. If you like *leading others*, create an online group where you lead and offer a lot of value. The group becomes a sales funnel.

If you would like more in-depth help crafting your stories, *The Career Stories Method*, by Kerri Twigg is an excellent book. Kerri's index card method is an example activity in her book. It is a simple and effective way to begin building your stories. Kerri also shared this method in my bestselling career book, *YouMap*.

Avoid thinking of each marketing effort as a transactional tit for tat. An example is writing a social media post and expecting a direct contact from a prospective client in response. Consistent marketing efforts establish you as the go-to person in your niche. The goal is for you to be at the top of people's mind when they talk to someone who needs what you do best.

Consumers of your content won't always be your customers, but they can still be your *ambassadors*. Many hands make light work. The more people motivated and equipped to tell others about you, the better. Ambassadors are the path to a referral-based business where other people send clients your way instead of you having to continually find them.

Judi: When I began consulting, I would identify potential

clients, especially in the non-profit world, and offer them something of significant value pro bono. One of two things happened. We did the pro-bono work, and they asked me to continue on a paying basis. Or they were so excited about what I was willing to give them, they figured what we offer for sale must be even better, and they became paying clients. Some of those organizations I've worked with for over 20 years and they continue to refer my services. That's a terrific way to create "ambassadors."

Hopefully, ambassadors will be sending clients your way, and then you'll need help with client contracts. Let's cover contracts next.

10

————— ⚬ℨ —————

CLIENT SERVICE CONTRACTS
Judi

In an ideal world we wouldn't need contracts. Even within a trusted partnership, misunderstandings happen.

You might receive differing advice about the need for contracts based on who you ask. Detail-oriented people might recommend hiring a lawyer to create a thorough contract that anticipates each scenario that could arise.

Others might recommend simply addressing roles and expectations in the discovery call conversation where you cover what to expect from one another in the engagement and any relevant policies.

We fall somewhere in the middle of this advice. A reliable way to reduce misunderstandings and align your expectations to your clients' is to have an agreement *in writing*. Your agreement doesn't need to be formal and full of complicated legal jargon. In fact, you can even embed your service agreement into the proposal you send to prospects.

If you're already working with clients and are not using client service contracts or detailed proposals with clear service terms and conditions, it's not too late to start. We suggest putting the scope of the work into a document as the best way to show you are a professional and work in a business-like way. Often, larger clients will take your proposal and turn it into a contract you can sign.

If having a proposal and a contract seems like overkill to you, an alternative is to put a statement of acceptance at the bottom of the proposal with a place for your customer to sign and date. This can function as a contract.

In 25 years of coaching, I have never had a client fail to pay their invoice. And I've only had two experiences where clients wanted a refund.

In the first instance, a significant change in responsibility left the person realizing at that time the coaching engagement was not possible. In the second experience, "Dad" wanted the project more than his daughter, and so although she was a working professional, he had intervened inappropriately in terms of the scope of the engagement. I offered a full refund, which she declined. She offered a more than fair settlement for what we did in the first phase and we parted cordially.

Given that I have worked with more than 50,000 people, I would say putting things in writing definitely helps minimize misunderstandings and ensure payment.

One last thing. At the end of all my proposals I put this short paragraph:

Coaching is a highly personal relationship, and we recognize that circumstances change. (Client name) and (Client organization) are under no obligation to complete all the coaching services detailed in this proposal. (Client name) is free to leave the engagement at any time with no financial penalty. (Client organization) will only be charged for work that is completed. This proposal is for information only and the proposal elements may change or be re-ordered, depending on what (client name) wants to accomplish. Any changes that incur added costs will be submitted in writing for approval and will become an amendment to the contract.

In the next chapter, *Proposals*, we will review a sample proposal and share important considerations when creating them.

11

❦

PROPOSALS
Kristin

Proposals are an effective tool to induce prospective clients to engage your services. When I was coaching individuals, my assistant quickly followed up the discovery call with a proposal. Following up as soon as possible after a discovery call or initial conversation is essential. A prospect's interest is at its highest right after speaking with you, and their enthusiasm will only wane with each day that passes.

In our follow up email, we supplied a de-identified sample client report to generate intrigue and interest, reiteration of select important terms such as methods of payment accepted and payment terms, and a call to action to request changes to the engagement or confirm acceptance of the proposed services. See "Chapter 18: Discovery Calls" for more on effective discovery call management.

Following is an example of a simple proposal. A basic proposal should include the purpose, the process, and the fees. I have also noted other proposal considerations below the sample.

Coaching Plan – Client Name – Month/Year

Purpose: Outcomes a client can expect from the engagement.

Coaching Packages:

Premium – *Full coaching program package*

Process: List specifics of what the offering includes such as assessments and duration and number of sessions.

Example:

> *Phase 1*: Three one-hour sessions to uncover strengths, values, preferred skills, and interests
>
> *Phase 2*: Resume and LinkedIn profile creation
>
> *Phase 3*: 60-minute interview preparation session

Gold – *Mini coaching package*

Process: List specifics so clients see what they will not receive if they opt for this package over the premium package.

Example:

> *Phase 1*: Three one-hour sessions to uncover strengths, values, preferred skills, and interests
>
> *Phase 2*: Resume and LinkedIn profile creation

Basic – *One coaching (or consulting) hour*

Process: List specifics so clients see what they will not receive if they opt for this package over the others.

Example:

> One 60-minute session to provide a high-level debrief of YouMap® assessment results.

Fees:

SERVICES	FEE	TERMS
Premium	$ 1,999	50% down; 50% at conclusion -List any other terms
Gold	$899	50% down; 50% at conclusion -List any other terms
Basic	$349	Payable in full up front -List any other terms

ADDITIONAL FACTORS TO CONSIDER

- Decide if you require clients to pay for the entire program if they don't complete some of the services.

- State your refund policy, even if the policy is no refunds. Include refund specifics as a footnote in the document or below the table outlining fees and terms. Will refunds be limited to coaching fees and exclude expenses you have incurred, such as assessment costs? See Judi's sample paragraph at the end of her proposals outlined in the previous chapter, "Client Contracts."

- Specify how many edits, reviews or revisions are included in your services. For example, if you write resumes, you might include two edits after the final version is delivered, or within a set period of time, such as 30 days.

- Explicitly indicate that no changes that incur additional costs will be added without the client's written approval to avoid "scope creep." If unfamiliar with the term scope creep, this means additional services are added to a project without the price or timeline adjusted to account for the additions. You risk not being paid if you add scope to a project that is not outlined in the client's original fee schedule. You will be short-changed if a client adds scope to the engagement without an adjustment to your fee.

- Note how long your quoted fee is honored, such as three, six, or twelve months from the date sent to the client.

- Explicitly state expectations of the client's participation to receive the best results. Are there exercises or assignments the client must complete? Indicate results rely on both coach and client fulfilling their roles in the engagement.

- Indicate the engagement will begin once the deposit, or full payment, is received.

- Indicate the timeline in which coaching hours must be used, such as six months from the engagement onset.

- When sending the proposal, prompt the prospective client to advise if he wishes to add or remove services, or does not wish to continue at this time. If he would like to move forward, you can ask him to respond to the email showing acceptance of the proposal and terms. Alternatively, you can have the client sign the proposal using document signing software or simply signing, scanning, and sending the signed proposal to you.

More important than including every fine detail in a proposal is writing one that is easy to follow. If you are a detail-oriented person, include a digestible summary of the proposal at the top, similar to what is shown in this chapter.

If a client has a good feeling about working with you in the discovery call, don't change his or her mind by making the client trudge through a cumbersome proposal. The proposal should be a formality after a discovery call.

Remember, *confused people won't say yes*. Reduce friction and make it easy for people to quickly size up the proposal and move forward with the coaching. Of course, if you haven't quite nailed down your services and pricing, keep reading. We cover this in the next chapter.

12

☙

SERVICES & PRICING

Kristin

As a general rule, your pricing strategy should be based on the project and value that project delivers, not by the hour. Pricing services using an hourly model often results in under-charging and over-working because your pre-work and post-work end up being on your own dime. We must consider added pre-work and post-work time spent when the client isn't present, as well as the overall return on investment a client receives from our expertise.

For example, I hired a professional speaker to present to the YouMap® coach community at our annual gala. The speaker fee was $5,000. She attended the 90-minute event, spoke and answered questions for one hour during the 90-minute period. She was worth every dollar, and the feedback was superb.

I don't view the speaker's fee in terms of hours. I did not pay $5,000 *per hour*. I paid $5,000 for valuable expertise that will generate additional revenue for my business and the businesses of the coaches.

Imagine if the speaker, who has decades of successful consulting experience with clients such as NASA, charged a measly $250 for the hour she spoke at the event. Then let's say I implement six strategies this expert outlined to scale my business impact. As a direct result of implementing these new strategies, the number of enrolled coaches in my coaching certification program increases by a mere 10 additional coaches over the course of the year. The revenue generated is $23,000.

A professional who has built valuable knowledge over her career should not receive $250 in compensation to show up and impart hard-earned wisdom that will bring me $23,000 in revenue. Makes sense, right? Paying $5,000 is money well spent and money she deserves.

Now, if I purchased that same speaker's books and made a killing implementing her advice, that's a different story. Book sales are passive income where the author's presence is not required.

An hour of your time and expertise is more valuable to those who need it than you are probably charging for it.

To avoid being paid by the hour, I recommend creating packages. Think about your ideal client. What does she need in a comprehensive package? Present your comprehensive package as a top tier offering. Give your packages a title to reinforce their level of value rather than assigning *Option 1* or *Package 1*. Some examples are *Platinum*, *Elite*, or *Premium*.

Your middle package could have names such as *Gold*, *Plus*, or *Economy*. Your bottom package could have names such as *Silver*, *Regular*, or *Basic*.

A word of caution on creating too many packages. It might seem wise to produce every combination of offerings, but human psychology says that's not a solid strategy.

THE PARADOX OF CHOICE

The book, *The Paradox of Choice: Why Less is More* by Barry Schwartz, explains why too many choices causes anxiety in consumers.

The paradox of choice is an observation that when people have too many options to choose from, rather than feeling delighted and assured they will get what they want, the added options induce stress and complicate decision-making. Consequently, the customer simply doesn't make a choice.

Imagine taking a five-year-old child to a toy store and telling him that grandma gave him spending money for his birthday and he can choose any toy he wants.

Now, imagine offering the child three toy options and telling him to choose one of the three toys to take home.

Which scenario would result in a faster, easier decision?

You probably know the answer from experience. I once tried to buy a crockpot for a friend. When I arrived at the store, there were approximately fifteen crockpots to choose from. I grew weary as I read the details on each box. So many details! I didn't even know what some of the features were. I left the store without a crockpot.

Confused people won't say yes.

When structuring your packages, include a brief, clear summary of the package at the top, with clear details below for those who want them.

If needed, list any à la carte add-on options in a separate list below your 2-3 package options. Make it simple for your customer to see what your packages include and exclude. You don't want a customer to have to sift through the package explanations to figure out the differences between them. A simple checklist, like this one, will help:

Services Included	Silver	Gold (most popular)	Platinum
Apple	☑	☑	☑
Orange	☑	☑	☑
Pear		☑	☑
Banana			☑
Corn			☑
Fee	$799	$999	$1,199

You'll notice the Gold package is flagged as *most popular*. Many people tend to have a thought process something like this when spending money:

> *Well, I don't want a cheap, lower quality choice. I won't get the results I want. And I don't need to spend quite so much on the top tier package. That's a bit extravagant. So, I'll go with the middle choice!*

THE CENTER STAGE EFFECT

A well-researched psychological phenomenon, known as the center stage effect, is that people have a bias for choosing middle options, and this isn't solely related to pricing. Retailers found when they moved toothbrushes from a top shelf to the middle shelf, sales increased by eight percent.[7]

Knowing this, you should set up your middle package as the one you want to sell most often at the fee you want to earn for an engagement. Base the price of the lower and higher packages off the middle package.

One or more services should be *added* to the middle package to create the top tier offering. Then, *remove* one or more services from the middle package to create the bottom tier offering. This approach makes building the packages simpler, with your main effort on building out the middle package.

Keep in mind, it isn't necessary to offer multiple packages. If you're clear on who you serve and what they need, you can certainly have one signature offering and only serve clients who want that complete offering. Just remember, you won't have the advantage of the center stage effect.

If your clients have too many individualized needs for one package, or clients aren't hiring you, evaluate using a tiered package strategy to test if you get better results converting prospects to clients.

WHAT SHOULD I CHARGE?

I received advice from an experienced coach when I was first starting my business who said if more than 20 percent of prospects are not converting to clients, you are overcharging or not making your value clear in the mind of the buyer. Conversely:

If more than 80 percent of clients accept your proposals, you're not charging enough.

Pricing services can be nerve wracking for new coaches. Comparing what coaches in your region charge is one place to start. For example, if I go to thumbtack.com and enter my zip code and the kind of coach I'm seeking, a list of coaches and their rates are displayed. In addition, the information includes a customer rating and how many times they've been hired on thumbtack. What is the average or most common fee in your area?

A constant tension exists between needing to bring in revenue while also being afraid a customer will walk away. Escaping this requires a mental shift around money. First, you want to avoid clients whose primary concerns are about cost. It's understandable that most people want to get the most for their money. No one wants to waste their time and money.

When a client is hung up on the cost, or asks if you'll accept a lower fee, you can share that in your experience, to provide a high-quality product or experiences that clients are happy with, the current price is what works best. I received this advice from my friend Bob and it works well. If the price conscious customer walks away, you're better off. Remember, not all customers are good customers. Someone who doesn't see the value in what you're offering will end up on your difficult clients list.

Judi: One more thought. When you are having an exploratory conversation with a prospective client, it doesn't hurt to offer a "preview" of what your services cost. For example, if s/he likes some of your suggestions as to what the engagement might include, you can tell him or her the approximate cost, explaining it might be a bit lower or a bit more depending on the final agreement. Ask if this is a price range with which s/he is comfortable.

PAYMENT PLANS

Offering payment plans is a way to help clients bridge the gap to enable them to hire you. You might offer 50 percent down and 50 percent thirty days later or at the end of the engagement. Make certain not to start the work until you've received a down payment. You want to pay for assessments and other out-of-pocket costs with the client's funds not funds from your own account.

DELINQUENT PAYMENTS

One irritation of self-employment is a customer who won't pay your invoice. As mentioned, I recommend requiring a 50 percent down payment of the total fee before any work commences. I've had a small number of clients fail to pay their balance and successfully obtained payment in all but a handful of cases.

You have several courses of action for delinquent payments. If a client is late paying an initial deposit, you can terminate the relationship or the specific project. Consider adding payment due dates to your proposals and state that services will be canceled or rescheduled if a deposit is not received by the due date.

It's a good idea to set up automated payment reminder emails for unpaid invoices. However, emails are easy to ignore. After a set number of reminders, change your method of contact. Get the client on the phone. If collections conversations make you uncomfortable, delegate the task to a virtual assistant. When a client continues to avoid collection attempts, you can sell the debt to a collection agency or take the client to small claims court, depending on the size of the debt. For small invoices, taking a client to court won't be worth the hassle.

If a client is a repeat customer, stop offering services on credit and require payment in full before work begins. You can build late payment penalties into contracts or proposals and require customers read and sign it to accept the policy.

Ultimately, if a client defaults on payment you will write unpaid invoices off as bad debts on your taxes.

SLIDING SCALE FEES

Judi: Coaches and consultants sometimes choose to use a sliding scale for their fees. Sliding scale fees are prices that vary based on the experience or income level of the client. Some business coaches recommend against this practice, but it might be right for you.

A sliding scale creates accessibility for more people. Others charge higher fees to executives and organizations to fund pro bono non-profit work. For example, you would be able to fund out-of-pocket assessment costs, travel, and your time through a sliding scale method.

SEEK TO ADD VALUE

An ambitious career changer once contacted me for coaching, yet my pricing didn't fit her budget. She saved her money to be able to afford my coaching fee and contacted me a year later to begin. When you know your value, and others do too, clients tend to become less price conscious.

A friend once told me customers must feel they've earned $1.20 in value for every dollar they spend with you. *Always have a mindset of creating added value for your clients.*

✑ ACTIVITY:

Brainstorm ways to add value to clients without added costs to you such as practical resources you can provide. For example, if you had a resume writing service, you could offer toolkits in your client packages with networking tips, a job application tracker, interview preparation kit, etc.

_____

_____

_____

_____

_____

_____

Another excellent way to increase your package pricing while adding more value for your clients is to incorporate assessments into your coaching. We cover assessments in "Chapter 20: Assessments & Tools."

In the next chapter, we will discuss finding your niche, and what to do if you are interested in more than one.

13

NICHES

Kristin

To niche, or not to niche. That is the question on the lips of coaches. Sam Walton, founder of Walmart, once said, "If everybody is doing it one way, there's a good chance you can find your niche by going exactly in the opposite direction."

Permit me to make a slight adjustment to Walton's sentiment. Rather than going in an opposite direction, take the path others can't easily take as well. In other words, there are things you do best which the market needs that other coaches can't exactly replicate. That which is unique to you is your market differentiation.

Before we go too deep, let's take pressure off you. Don't tie yourself in knots trying to find a niche. Sometimes the way to discover your niche is through exploration or trial and error. When I transitioned from executive to career coaching, I offered the complete gamut of services from career discovery through interview preparation, and everything in between.

One time, I had a client purchase two job search strategy sessions. After the first session ended the client said, "That wasn't what I was expecting. Could I have a refund for the second session?" I felt bad for the client and also embarrassed. Yet, I know that I dreaded certain kinds of engagements. Job search strategy was one of those. We don't want to build an army of people who received services we didn't enjoy providing. Those clients are unlikely to be our ambassadors.

I started paying more attention to work I enjoyed most where clients experienced excellent outcomes. Here are three questions I used for reflection as I assessed and explored:

What services do I feel confident delivering?

What client deliverables cause me to procrastinate?

Which client engagements energize me?

My tops strengths are:

Maximizer – moves people into roles where their greatest potential can be lived out.

Strategic – Faced with a variety of options, can easily find the best path to a goal.

Ideation – Able to find connections between disparate phenomena.

Futuristic – Imaginative, creative, visionary; inspires others with visions of the future and can identify the stepping stones to get there.

Input – Curious and resourceful; acquires and collects information, facts, and data to use and share.

These top strengths are in the *influencing* and *thinking* domains, which means I prefer to think up ideas (*Ideation*) to create a vision with a client (*Futuristic*), develop a strategy to bring the vision to reality (*Strategic*), which is supported by any needed resources (*Input*).

Lastly, my *influencing* strength, *Maximizer*, works to move others to action and into roles which realize their full potential.

I have no *executing* strengths in my top 20 CliftonStrength themes. As you can imagine, our strengths influence the services that feel energizing and effortless, and those that feel like drudgery. Writing resumes and job search coaching brought me no joy. I especially procrastinated on resumes, even though I was good at writing them. I often had a headache or felt emotionally and physically depleted after writing a resume.

However, when I would meet someone who had no idea what they wanted to do with their life, I was absolutely energized. Finally, a puzzle I can help solve that will move this person in a direction where they will shine. Now *that* was motivating!

Judi: Kristin and I are wired similarly in our strengths, which makes sense since she's my daughter.

My tops strengths are:

Maximizer – *moves people into roles where their greatest potential can be lived out.*

Strategic – *Faced with a variety of options, can easily find the best path to a goal.*

Futuristic – *Imaginative, creative, visionary; inspires others with visions of the future and can identify the stepping stones to get there.*

Activator – *Makes things happen by turning thoughts into actions.*

Input – *Curious and resourceful; acquires and collects information, facts, and data to use and share.*

These strengths have helped me specialize in three distinct kinds of executive coaching engagements that I most enjoy: high performance, high potential, and intervention coaching. That's all that I do.

I start with data. My Input *strength leads me to ask questions and leverage assessments and tools to gain insights, creating a clear picture of the person I'm working with. My* Futuristic *theme helps me discover the hopes and dreams of my clients and co-create a vision of where they want to go.*

I use my Strategic *nature to quickly figure out how to help my clients get from where they are to where they want to be. Sometimes that change is a role, and sometimes the change is within them. My* Maximizer *drives me to help steer them to places where they will be most effective, and my* Activator *theme influences people to act on the steps we've produced together.*

I will share more about this kind of work in "Chapter 19: Coaching Process & Best Practices" and will walk you through the steps of my coaching engagements.

I meet a lot of coaches who perform services because they feel they must, even if they have no interest in them or downright despise the work. I meet a lot of career coaches who write resumes and hate it. If a client is going to transition careers, she will need a resume. Yet, that resume doesn't have to be written by that coach if he doesn't enjoy writing them.

When I was career coaching, I created partnerships with resume writers to take over once my client's goal was set. This approach was a win/win/win. I no longer felt drained, the client got what they needed from people motivated and skilled to provide it, and the resume writer didn't have to drum up the client or start from nothing since I supplied a "fast-forward" based on the coaching work we had already done. The resume writers also sent clients my way that needed coaching before a resume was written – a reciprocal referral opportunity.

When you perform services you enjoy where you are also skilled, you delight your customers and create ambassadors to refer more clients who energize you. When you offer services you dislike, but you're skilled doing, you create referrals that bring you misery. Ugh. When you perform services you dislike and are also not highly skilled, you damage your reputation. Double ugh.

In "Chapter 4: Your Ideal Clients," I walked you through defining *who* you want to help. That chapter is foundational before you focus on a niche. Your niche drills down into *how* you want to help your target clients. If you don't know *who* you want to help you're not quite ready to think about *how* you help.

For example, you might know your ideal clients are men in their 50's or 60's who are contemplating their final career move. After thinking about a niche, you might decide to focus on tradesmen who need to find viable work options that are easier on their work-worn bodies.

"Chapter 2: You, the Coach," is an important chapter to work through prior to narrowing your niche because it uncovers your unique advantages based on *The Four Pillars of Career Fit*™. No one is wired like you with your exact set of experiences. That is an important consideration when choosing a niche.

After going through the reflection and discovery exercises in the book, you might feel a pull toward more than one niche. What then?

CREATING A SERVICE UMBRELLA

Amoreena, introduced in "Chapter 1: Coach Stories," is a YouMap® coach (who has since become a YouMap® Master Trainer) and was reimagining her business focus while going through the certification program. At that time, she was working with unemployed coalminers to help them transition to a new industry and, as she described it, stop eating and drinking their feelings.

She shared she also had a desire to use YouMap® in relationship coaching to help couples understand one another better.

You have seen the "energy healer/real estate agent/entrepreneur coach/LinkedIn trainer" profile online that feels scattered. It might appear these multi-faceted coaches are trying to cover their bases to increase their potential client base, or they simply have varied interests and have not found a common thread for packaging their services in an understandable way.

When we try to appeal to so many people, we end up appealing to no one. Yet, that doesn't mean you can't have different services for different clients. One approach is employing a service umbrella strategy. Umbrella branding is common in the product world. Examples of companies who employ umbrella branding are Johnson & Johnson, Proctor & Gamble, and Unilever. Did you know Unilever owns Ben & Jerry's and Lifebuoy hand sanitizer? Ice cream and hand sanitizer might seem like strange bedfellows.

Unilever says their purpose is to make sustainable living commonplace. As one of the largest consumer goods companies, that overarching purpose creates the umbrella for them to do business across multiple brands to build and scale their global footprint.

As a service provider, you can create a purpose-based container, or umbrella, for your services too. Let's go back to Amoreena's example when she shared her interest in relationship coaching and career coaching. I suggested a service umbrella for her as two related pillars: *Helping people gain fulfillment in two key areas of life* – relationships and career.

Your branding should reveal and speak to the intersection of your services. In Amoreena's case, these two areas of life are often considered most important and intersect significantly with each other. If your career is going well but you're struggling in your marriage, the career could end up opening an outlet to avoid your home life. Conversely, if you are miserable at work, there is potential for that misery to seep into your personal life and affect your relationships at home.

By positioning the *why* behind connecting unrelated offerings, you create a service umbrella that makes sense to people. Amoreena found when talking to men that their primary concern was finding love and connection, even though they initially sought her out for financial and career concerns.

If you have the experience, skillset, tools, credibility, and interest to serve multiple needs, consider creating a service umbrella to house your offerings. Speak about your services using unified and connected language that explain why you focus on these areas, and how they are related, to avoid the appearance of randomness to potential customers.

Life often requires trial and error. Finding your niche is no different. "The 3 C's of Coaching" section in "Chapter 2:

You, the Coach," is a solid starting point for exploring your niche. You want to coach what you know, combine what you know what your abilities (strengths and skills) and care deeply about the work. If you haven't done those exercises, that is a good next step to narrowing down your niche. Refer to your *Coach Canvas*, also explained in Chapter 2, for inspiration.

If targeting your niche is causing unnecessary pressure, open yourself to the process of discovery. As long as you have awareness of your strengths, values, preferred skills and personality-based interests, you will know you are exploring in the right territory.

I like to use a Disney World trip analogy. Some people prefer to enjoy the Disney® experience by exploring with a spontaneous approach instead of following a strict itinerary. All they need is to confirm they're inside Disney and not, for example, in the Sahara Desert. If that describes your current approach to coaching, you can't go wrong exploring within the bounds of what you do best to find out what you enjoy most.

Okay, after you've found your niche, let's get some clients!

14

⸺ ⚹ ⸺

ATTRACT CLIENTS
Kristin

When I began career coaching I asked everyone I met if they were satisfied in their work. I encouraged people to talk about themselves as I listened. This provided an opportunity to serve others by sharing expertise based on what they chose to share with me.

These organic conversations were not manipulation or cramming my services down the throats of people who crossed my path. I simply created opportunities to help people every chance I could get.

Both Judi and I genuinely enjoy making a difference in people's lives and are passionate about coaching. The intersection of these two things create natural, authentic conversations built on trust and credibility. These encounters often lead to either a coaching engagement with the person directly or to the individual referring us to others who need the services we provide.

When you're enthusiastic about your work, you can't help but share your knowledge with others. When you genuinely show interest in people, you are more likely to get and keep their attention. A lack of desire to serve others or a primary interest in making a sale will be detected by most people. Along with the above example, you have many options for securing clients, including some you might not have considered. Let's start with lead generation.

LEAD GENERATION

Essentially, lead generation is finding target clients and directly contacting them regarding your services. If you haven't launched a business, your immediate network is where you should start looking for clients because you have established relationships. Craft a communication such as a blog post or email that shares your new business venture, and send it to people you trust in your network:

- Former co-workers or managers
- Family members
- Friends
- Fellow club members

In "Chapter 4: Your Ideal Clients," I included an exercise under "Your Immediate Network" to help reveal ideal clients. To prevent you from having to hunt for it, I have provided the prompt below. You can use this prompt to create a list of potential first clients:

List specific people you can think of who could be helped by your services or products, including people you've helped who might welcome being an ambassador. Why might they be interested?

Examples are people with whom you volunteer, share hobbies, or go to church. Others include alumni or professors from your academic institution, past or present coworkers you trust, friends and extended family, fellow members of professional associations or clubs, mentors or business contacts, former and current clients.

If you have a social media presence that states you are a coach, consultant, or business owner, be prepared to receive relentless connection requests from "Lead Generation" providers who want you to hire them to get clients for you. If you accept the connection request, you will likely receive an immediate direct message with a sales pitch.

Many social media sales pitches are automated. My name on LinkedIn is displayed as "KRISTIN A. SHERRY." When I receive messages that begin, "Hello KRISTIN A.," with my name capitalized and middle initial included, I know I received an automated sales message. I disconnect immediately because my connections might accept a connection request because I am linked to the individual.

Personally, I do not hire lead generation providers. Consider this question: "Is the experience of cold sales pitches one you want your prospective clients to have from a lead generation specialist operating on your behalf?"

LEAD GENERATION THROUGH GENEROSITY

Judi: Early in my consulting career I was a graduate of Leadership Buffalo, and I saw a missing piece in orientation. I went back to the Executive Director and the Board Chair and said I think we should add an assessment to the process. They thought it was a great idea but said they couldn't afford it. I told them, "No problem. I'll donate it." I donated all the assessments and also facilitation of a workshop for those fifty people. I did this for three years running.

In those three years I gained so many new clients. The people who participated in Leadership Buffalo then came to me and said, "I want you to come do this at my company."

When you're strategic about the audience you donate to it will often create more business leads. I wanted to give because I wanted to make a difference, but it also allowed me to build my reputation and my business.

If you are fortunate enough to start working with an organization with annual revenue of $500 million or more, this can easily be a six-figure client for you in less than two years! So, think about how you can retain (or gain) clients by offering additional help to them.

I hope Judi's story sparks ideas for using lead generation combined with generosity to build relationships and grow your business.

What if the idea of proactive lead generation and outreach makes you feel anxious? You might even be second guessing your ability to bring in clients or have a sustainable coaching practice. You might be asking, "How can I draw people to me?" Perhaps a softer approach to selling is what you prefer.

Soft Selling

You absolutely can build a coaching practice without aggressive lead generation and sales pitching. Every coach is wired differently according to their *Four Pillars of Career Fit*™. So, in this next section, we'll focus on softer approaches to selling to help you build your client base. In "Chapter 4: Your Ideal Clients," I walked you through defining your client target. In this section, I want to help you attract desirable individuals *within* your ideal clients.

For example, you might want to work with women in career transition, but you are keen to avoid women who make excuses or aren't self-motivated. Why does this matter? If you communicate with intention to attract individuals you want to work with, and repel those you don't, you can reduce time spent on exploratory calls with someone who isn't a good fit.

The most effective way to not only attract clients, but attract the *right* clients, is to speak your strengths in all you do. If this sounds ambiguous or odd, don't worry. I will lay this out for you.

Sheri was experiencing frustration with a client. Her client took a glass as half empty approach, focusing on limitations and problems. The client also procrastinated on completion of coaching exercises. One of Sheri's strengths is empathy, which led her to be confused about why she was frustrated and impatient with her client.

To better understand her frustration, let's review Sheri's strengths in the order of priority.

1. Accountable and dependable (*Responsibility* which is an *executing* strength).

2. Moving people to their potential (*Maximizer* which is an *influencing* strength).

3. Continuous improvement (*Learner* which is a *thinking* strength).

4. Productivity and efficiency (*Arranger* which is an *executing* strength).

5. Sensing the emotions of others (*Empathy* which is a *relationship-building* strength).

In "Chapter 2: You, the Coach," we emphasized that our strengths set our priorities every day. Since Sheri's top strength, *Responsibility*, is an *executing* strength, it explains her drive for results. In addition, this strength is oriented to do things correctly, ethically, and take ownership of the results.

Empathy is a supporting strength, which is not as strong as *Responsibility*. Sheri's empathy was eclipsed by the frustration caused by her client's procrastination, which prevented both of them from getting results!

Reviewing Sheri's other priorities, we also see she was unable to maximize her client (*Maximizer*) because he wasn't making forward progress, nor did she feel the coaching engagement was productive (*Arranger*). In short, multiple priorities were suppressed within this coach/client dynamic.

I explained to Sheri how to attract clients who best fit with her strengths, enabling her to supply the best possible results. First, I pointed out she is best suited to work with clients who are also highly accountable (*Responsibility*). The way to attract accountable clients is to use intentional language that causes a prospect to self-identify with your ideal client. For example:

"I work with highly accountable individuals who are ready to take ownership of a career transition, but…" I'll explain the "but" in the statement in a moment.

When conducting discovery calls, Sheri should outline her process, the time commitment needed, and that she collaborates best with clients who are motivated and dedicated to completing the requirements.

Once she has found a shared strength with potential clients, she can choose two things she does best that her clients need most. This is where the "but" comes in.

The complete statement might read something like this:

I work with **highly accountable** individuals who are ready to take **ownership** of a career transition but are **uncertain of their next career move** or **how to create a plan** to achieve it.

Uncertain of their next career move – Sheri's *Maximizer* strength equips her to effectively discover what a person can do best.

How to create a plan – Even a clear goal cannot be achieved if a person is uncertain about the steps to take to achieve it. Sheri's *Arranger* strength brings an organized flexibility that equips her to figure out how all the pieces and resources can be arranged to achieve a result. She is adept at figuring out the best way to get things done.

By using this specific language, Sheri can attract people who have the ability to follow through while she fills in the client's gaps with her other strengths that a client lacks.

Consider the clients you want to serve. What single shared priority is most important for your client based on your strengths? Do you want to work with people who are positive, achievement-oriented, curious and open-minded, focused, disciplined, action-oriented, enthusiastic?

One final example should help clarify this approach to attracting clients. My shared priority with clients comes from my top strength, *Maximizer*. I enjoy working with people who want to "go big or go home." They want to be at their best and live out their potential.

Once I've attracted other maximizers, I use the following three strengths to encourage clients and move them to action:

Strategic – Identifies best practical path for a client.

Futuristic – Co-creates a client vision.

Ideation – Conceptualizes the pathway to the vision.

ACTIVITY:

Choose a shared priority to look for in clients based on your strengths (Review your *Coach Canvas* for ideas). What strength would be ideal to share with your clients? (e.g. *Achiever, Harmony, Adaptability*.)

Reflect on two or three of your other strengths as your differentiators and how they will help your clients.

Bonus: Include one or two of your top values from your *Coach Canvas* into your messaging to attract like-minded clients.

_____

_____

_____

_____

_____

_____

_____

_____

 Keep yourself visible to attract the right clients. Some ideas are offering workshops or monthly webinars, speaking at events where your customers are present, and attending conferences.

Make a list of conversational questions to ask people in social situations to get them talking about themselves and what's frustrating them. In response, offer a few tips to show your knowledge without pitching or selling. Your good will can plant seeds that bear fruit in the future.

Once you've worked with clients, repeat business is the best business because it lessens the pressure of continually filling your customer pipeline. Are you leaving money on the table?

REPEAT BUSINESS

One of the best sources for generating new business opportunities are through current and former clients. Small Business Trends reports compelling data on why customer retention must be part of every business owner's growth strategy:

- The average repeat customer spends 67 percent more in the second and third years of their relationship with a business than they do in the first six months.[8]
- A five percent increase in customer retention can lead to an increase in profits of between 25 and 95 percent.[9]
- Repeat customers spend 33 percent more than new customers.[10]
- A 10 percent increase in customer retention levels results in a 30 percent increase in the value of the company.[11]

Periodic Outreach

Maintain a list of your best clients. When adding a new service offering, contact each client individually, rather than an impersonal email blast, using your preferred method of communication. Briefly introduce the offering and how it will help the client.

Example:

> Good morning, Jackie,
>
> I hope all is well since we worked together to land your Operations Manager role at J.T. Foods. I remember you mentioned you wished you knew your *Four Pillars of Career Fit*™ 20 years ago!
>
> I'm contacting you to share a new offering to help you better understand and support your team. I am now offering YouMap® team workshops! These workshops supply deeper insight into your team and empower you to increase employee satisfaction, job fit, and retention.
>
> Are you available next week to discuss how YouMap® can increase your team's effectiveness as it helped you?

High Quality Follow-up

At the end of each coaching engagement, let the client know other ways you help. Neglecting to convert existing clients into repeat clients is a way coaches, consultants and small businesses leave money on the table. Following are a few more ideas to avoid making this mistake:

- Develop post-coaching programs, and guide clients to join at the end of the formal coaching program. Offer existing clients discounted rates for signing on to an additional program.
- Offer discounted retainer rates at the end of an engagement such as a coaching maintenance package for support and accountability. You might include a weekly check-in and email support in the offering. For example, if you helped your client gain a promotion, lose weight, or career transition, a maintenance package can support her success in the new role, help to keep the weight off, or navigate unexpected challenges after a transition.
- Create a Mastermind group and invite clients to join an upcoming group at the end of the formal coaching program.
- Conduct monthly lunch and learns or webinars and offer monthly memberships or per session fees to attend.
- Set up a private Facebook group and invite clients to join for valuable content and to expand their network.
- Create a simple and straightforward summary of your offerings. A client might hire you for career

transition coaching and not realize you offer corporate workshops.

- Thank the client for choosing to work with you and proactively thank her for referring others who might need x, y, or z services. This is a wonderful time to briefly summarize ways you can help her network.
- Invite the client to contact you should her situation change or if she needs more help in the future.

Keep your end of engagement email *brief* but impactful. Prioritize important points at the top in case people don't read the entire email. It's also a good idea to ask clients if they would write a testimonial of your work on LinkedIn. Offer guidance to make it easy to say yes, such as, "What did you like about working with me? How was I most helpful to you?"

The best scenario is that repeat business will soon replace lead generation. In "Chapter 8: Financial Considerations," we mentioned Angelique Rewers. She is brilliant at client retention and repeat customer business, so follow her.

SOCIAL MEDIA

Social media is an effective tool for attracting clients, provided you don't let it consume your time. I will share more on creating effective social media content in "Chapter 9: Messaging & Marketing." Here, I'll lay some groundwork by sharing my thoughts on social media as someone who has both used it heavily and taken lengthy sabbaticals away from it.

A common misperception among self-employed coaches and consultants is that you are bound to spend many hours on social media each day to build a business, becoming a social media squatter.

I train a lot of coaches, and many of them have, with overwhelming relief, celebrated the idea you can build and run a business without chaining yourself to social media.

I facilitate a monthly meeting of the minds for YouMap® coaches. At a recent meeting, I shared I had been on a sabbatical from LinkedIn to spend focused time in other areas of life. After the meeting, I received an email from one of the coaches, and this is how she responded:

> Thank you for leading by example. I have been engaging more on LI [LinkedIn] lately and find it tiresome most days. My fave thing to do is just keep doing right by my clients and they send me those near and dear to them. Seeing you be able to pivot to children's books, always discerning what is authentic to you and how you want to serve next inspires me to keep being true to myself as a professional and not follow the herd.

Holistically successful people are not on social media all day. Think of people who have reached a level of success in their industry that you admire. Do you believe they spend hours of their valuable time scrolling LinkedIn? I admire the work of Brené Brown, and despite having millions of followers on social media, I can't imagine her parked on her phone or computer for hours, posting and scrolling the newsfeed.

I could be wrong.

Though, somehow I think Ms. Brown spends more time building relationships in real time. The following quote from her TEDx Talk, *The Power of Vulnerability*, gives me this impression:

> *"Social media are great for developing community, but for true belonging, real connection and real empathy require meeting real people in a real space in real time." – Brené Brown*

If you're starting a business, you might think you need to be on social media all the time to drum up business. What is your impression of business owners who are continually online?

Do they have many clients or meaningful projects? How could they be busy if social media is dominating their time? Scrolling and responding to social media notifications is reactive. Being proactive is what leads to success. Do you need to adjust your social media time? If so, what will you do? List three changes you will make today:

1. _____

2. _____

3. _____

In addition to finding balance on social media, a common issue for coaches is giving away too many services for free. As you attract more people, you will experience an increase of people asking for free help. This can be a tricky issue for coaches to navigate; they tend to be natural helpers. We hope this next chapter on balancing generosity and profit is helpful.

15

---⚬---

BALANCE
GENEROSITY & PROFIT

Kristin

One topic coaches seem to struggle with most is balancing generosity with making a profit. A common denominator based on hundreds of conversations with coaches explained one key struggle to achieve profitability: *no pro bono guidelines were put in place.*

The difficulty of placing healthy parameters around pro bono services, plus the added expectation from others to receive free help is not unique to coaching.

If you have a techie in your family, who does everyone in the extended family call for computer advice or troubleshooting? Doctors and lawyers know this all too well. The expectation of free help tends to be most often placed on service professionals.

Those with expertise and experience are called on to dole out free advice far more than those selling a physical product. People are less likely to perceive any tangible costs associated with services. Yet, there are costs. Namely, time and opportunity.

Before going further, let's put a stake in the ground to state generosity is important. Any successful business owner should practice generosity. My best friend, Kimberly, has generosity in her top 10 values. Few things drive her up a wall more than a selfish and stingy person. Quite frankly, if you're in the coaching business, you can't afford to be stingy. Who wants to hire any service provider who isn't generous?

Time is one of your most valuable resources and, unlike a product which can be returned, you won't be able to get a refund on your time. Learning this lesson the hard way taught us to be *strategically* generous. We have found ways to give without tying our time to it. In this chapter, we'll show you tips to remain generous without jeopardizing the sustainability of your business.

Judi: I started out as a consultant. I didn't really become a coach until my fourth year in business. However, I had previously been a public affairs professional, and I knew many people in the Western New York community. So as my business grew, I developed the concept of helping one non-profit business annually pro bono.

At the onset, I chose non-profits that were doing something I valued. The United Way and Child & Family Services are examples of non-profits I helped. I settled on a dollar amount I was willing to give and let them choose what they wanted to use that for – coaching for an individual, one or two workshops, or a mix of services. At the end of the year, I could point to a lengthy list of benefits for my business as well as the organization:

- *Made new friends*
- *Helped people in the organization to increase their effectiveness – often far more than the organization expected*
- *Helped the organization solve problems they had not thought of asking me about*
- *Grew my reputation*
- *Created new tools or processes for the project and turned them into templates others would pay for*
- *Learned new things – often this was "research"*

Realistically, you can't give everything away to everyone who asks and expect to financially stay afloat. Setting parameters will help make decisions easier.

If you are compelled to give everything away for free, consider setting up a non-for-profit charity instead of a business. The following are other ideas to balance generosity and profit.

CREATE TIME-FREE FREEBIES

A time-free freebie is a form of tool, resource, or aid you can supply to help someone *without being present*. The only time associated with a time-free freebie is the one-time upfront investment to create it. Time-free freebies are a win/win. Below are some examples:

Blog articles – Write a handful of blogs or articles on your most commonly sought-after expertise and keep the links accessible for easy sharing. When asked for free help, share the right article.

Videos – Similar to the blog articles, create several short videos that offer do-it-yourself guidance. For example, if you are a career coach and you're often asked to review resumes, you could do a resume critique walkthrough showing someone how to critically evaluate each section of their resume. Drop these videos on YouTube if you are looking to monetize your channel.

Work samples – Consider creating some de-identified sample products to offer guidance. Sometimes people just need to see an example and can change an example to meet their needs.

FAQ documents – Are you answering the same questions repeatedly? Drop them into an FAQ and when those familiar questions inevitably come, drop a link to the resource.

Coaching prompts – Do people come to you with problems which prompt you to ask a certain set of questions to help them gain clarity? Create a slick one-page document with your branding that asks these coaching questions with space for the person to record their responses.

Process flow charts/decision trees – People often seek help because they don't know what steps to take. For example, what are the steps to transition one's career? What are the steps to pursue full custody of a child? Create a flow chart that illustrates the path forward with decision trees. This saves time answering process questions.

eBooks – Create digital e-books to sell on your website. If you're asked to work for free, offer an alternative download of your e-book for $4.99. If a person is serious about receiving help, s/he should be open to a small investment to have skin in the game. (People don't value things that are free, anyway.) I've given away numerous codes (which I bought on Amazon) to download the Kindle version of *YouMap*, my book on Amazon's Top 10 category bestseller list. Less than 50 percent of people download it upon receiving the free code. Do you believe people who won't take time to download a resource packed with the exact help they need will implement free advice I spend an hour sharing on a call?

Worksheets – Create coaching worksheets to guide people to DIY the solution they're looking for. For example, you could use worksheets to help people build accomplishment stories for a resume or to write their LinkedIn profile summary. A few instructions and some prompts and they will be on their way without your involvement!

5-MINUTE FAVORS

Wharton University business professor Adam Grant wrote about the five-minute favor in his book, *Give and Take: A Revolutionary Approach to Success*. Grant learned of the practice from entrepreneur Adam Rifkin.

A five-minute favor is the practice of allotting five minutes out of every day to do something that will help someone in your network without expecting anything in return.

Grant offers some suggestions on how to grant five-minute favors such as giving feedback, making introductions (ask permission first), giving an endorsement, supplying a resource, or sharing an idea.

When you make a habit of supplying value on a daily basis, you might find it easier to have boundaries about giving away your services for free.

You can use a five-minute rule of thumb, or time increment of your choice, to gauge when something is offered for free and when it becomes a paid service.

DISCOUNTS

Offering discounts is another way to be generous. Perhaps you'd like to offer discounts for certain groups such as military veterans. If you decide to offer a discount, define who is eligible to receive it.

Who is considered a friend or family? Does a friend of a friend count? Do military discounts include spouses or just the service member? Set criteria to make discounts easier to manage.

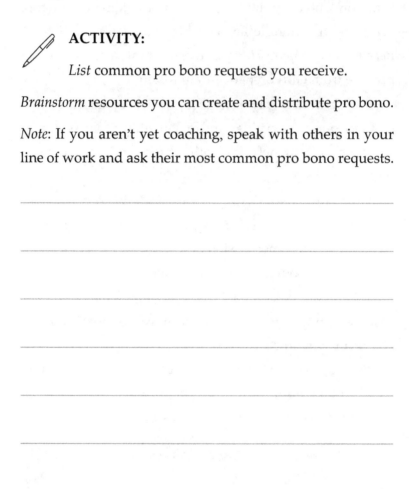

ACTIVITY:

List common pro bono requests you receive.

Brainstorm resources you can create and distribute pro bono.

Note: If you aren't yet coaching, speak with others in your line of work and ask their most common pro bono requests.

Requests For Free Or Discounted Services

Requests for free or discounted services are inevitable. You need not be offended by the request if you consider some cultures find this practice acceptable. It is expected in some cultures to supply your services to friends and family for free.

When someone asks for help or advice and you're not sure if the intention is to pay for your help, ask!

How can I best help you? Are you looking to engage my services, or are you seeking pro bono advice?

If the person wants to hire you, great! Proceed as usual by setting up a discovery call, sending an intake form, sending a proposal, or however you normally continue. If the person is seeking free help, you have several options on how to respond:

1. Indicate you only do pro bono work through the non-profit with which you volunteer and direct him or her to contact information.
2. Supply one of the resources you created that fits the need of the individual.
3. Refer the person to non-profits, websites, blogs, video content, podcasts, or other content creators that supply the kind of content the person is looking for.

If you don't wish to create pro bono resources, you can curate these to include non-profit sources, YouTube channels, and people you recommend following. For example, crossroadscareer.org is a non-profit that helps job seekers with free webinars, blog posts, a resume builder, job board, and career guides who offer free 45-minute calls to support those in need with resources and guidance.

Lastly, you can decline. Declines are due to one of four reasons:

1. You have all you can handle on your plate.
2. The request isn't your area of expertise.
3. You believe others are better suited to help.
4. You don't give away that much service for free.

 Create your responses for how you will manage free or discounted service requests so you are prepared and can quickly and easily handle these situations without guilt or stress.

Balancing generosity with making a profit enables you to afford to hire the help you need to run and grow your business. If support for your business is on your mind, head to the next chapter for steps you can take to find the right person for you and your practice.

16

————— ℭʒ —————

HIRE THE RIGHT ASSISTANT

Kristin

Our businesses cannot function optimally or grow without support.

One of my business regrets is waiting three years after starting it to hire an assistant. In hindsight, I struggled to entrust elements of my coaching practice to someone who wouldn't care about my clients as much as I did. I realize now that my attitude resulted in lost growth in earlier years because after I hired someone, my business grew to a new level.

I no longer send proposals or invoices. My time is invested in areas where I simply cannot quickly train another person to stand in my place, such as speaking, writing books, and innovating new products. I create a return on investment (ROI) when I spend time on value-added activities. Administration is not one of those activities, even though it is important for a business to run smoothly.

The time you spend generating invoices, creating proposals, and managing the administrative details of your business limit the time you are able to spend working *on* your business.

When I finally did hire an assistant, it was a client who needed a job. I trusted her, and so I hired her. I admittedly did not follow much of the advice I outline in this chapter with my first hire. I knew my client wasn't the best fit for the job, but, at the time, I prioritized meeting an employment need. My assistant was incredible with clients but struggled with organizational skills, details, time management, and follow up. These issues led me to manage more closely than I enjoy so I could catch errors and prevent important things from falling through the cracks.

Ultimately, these challenges were my responsibility, and I helped her find a new position before hiring someone else. I don't regret the decision to hire her. We did wonderful work together and are friends to this day. However, next time, I would not make an emotional decision. I learned from this experience and knew exactly what I needed in my next assistant.

I met my right hand, Mimi, at a career workshop at our church. She approached me after the session and expressed a desire to work with me to help her figure out the next step in her career. After we finished walking through her YouMap®, I realized Mimi was exactly who I needed to work alongside. She had relational strengths to connect well with clients and was also highly disciplined, organized, and process-minded.

We also shared values of connection, accountability, personal growth, making a difference in people's lives, living balanced lives, and feeling called to purpose-driven work. In addition, Mimi's YouMap® revealed our skills were complementary. Skills that were demotivating for me were listed on her profile as motivating and vice versa. As a result, we used the insights to align our roles with skills that bring out the best in both of us.

Lastly, Mimi had exactly what I needed from a personality-based interests perspective. She is a *helper* and an *organizer*, which is known as *The Caretaker*. Who better to support me than a caretaker? Mimi is helpful, efficient, trustworthy, productive, kind, loyal, and takes her responsibilities very seriously. She will also tactfully stand up for herself, which I love!

Working with Mimi has enabled me to invest significant effort to grow a global business while she keeps everything running smoothly. We make a truly exceptional team. Let's see to it that you get the Mimi you deserve.

In "Chapter 2: You, the Coach," you were introduced to *The Four Pillars of Career Fit*™. As a reminder, the four pillars are:

Strengths – Natural inherited talents
Values – What you consider most important
Skills – Abilities gained through experience
Personality – Traits and interests

Hiring an assistant to help you and your business thrive requires consideration of the Four Pillars, of both you and your assistant, as well as other considerations.

Research by Leadership IQ showed only 19 percent of new hires are an unequivocal success, with half failing in the first 18 months.[12] A bad hire is costly to a small business. I don't share this to cause you to fret about this decision. You can take intentional steps to save you pain.

HIRING PRE-WORK

Reflect and answer the following three questions:

#1: How will my assistant contribute to the mission of my business?

Have you ever watched an orchestra perform? Each musician is a highly skilled professional. Despite the level of skill of each individual, a conductor is necessary to keep every musician aligned to the conductor's mission, which might be a technically correct and emotionally moving experience that delights the audience.

The conductor supplies a common focal point for each member of the orchestra, regardless of the instrument they play. The same is true for employees you hire. Your mission enables those who work for you to prioritize, make decisions, organize their work, and deliver the results you expect, aligned to a set of values and operating principles.

What is the mission of your business? This should include the purpose of what you do, the values reflected in how you do it, and the goals you achieve for your clients. If you have created a business plan, you should have already completed this step. If not, the *Appendix* has a link to *The Small Business Start-up Guide* introduced in "Chapter 7: Starting a Business." Keep in mind, people you hire have been influenced by the culture and expectations of previous employers.

For example, let's say your new assistant previously worked in a customer service role. In that role, employees were rewarded for the number of calls they completed in a day, and the company encouraged completing calls in the shortest time possible. Customer service centered on efficiency and volume.

Perhaps you have fewer customers and are more concerned with a quality customer experience than volume and shorter call times. If you aren't clear on the mission of your business, you are unlikely to align your employees to support your business according to your expectations. Misalignment can result in various undesirable outcomes such as mistakes, productivity issues, inappropriate decisions, and customer dissatisfaction.

#2: What specific goals, deliverables, or expectations exist for my assistant now and in the future?

Two essential elements are represented in this question. First, you have goals, deliverables, and expectations for your assistant, even if you haven't taken the time to write them down. When we do not define our needs, we set others who support us up for failure. Our disappointment will always be based on hindsight. We will know we didn't get what we want when we see it, even if we did not set clear expectations up front. Even the most skilled assistant cannot read your mind.

Second, a small business can grow and change quickly. What are future considerations around how your business might expand or change? Will these changes require other skills that enable your assistant to grow with your business?

For example, when I first started my business, I focused solely on coaching individuals. As my business evolved and expanded, I added a product store for the general public to buy assessments for kids, teens and adults and a coaching certification program.

These new additions required an assistant who could manage customer service on a larger scale, as well as the coordination of an eight-week certification program. These new responsibilities were far more extensive than handling the details of a three-week coaching engagement for an individual client.

ACTIVITY:

Imagine your ideal assistant. What would a high performer look like?

Write a fictional story about your assistant doing a great job.

Why did you value the contribution?

What did your assistant deliver?

What are characteristics of *how* he delivered?

How did this help you and/or a customer?

Next, capture what your story reveals about what you need in an assistant in terms of their strengths, values, skills, and personality traits:

_____

_____

_____

_____

_____

_____

_____

After considering your mission, how your assistant will fit into your mission, and imagining your ideal assistant, you have a better foundation to define the skills and abilities you need in an assistant.

A good rule of thumb is to limit your list of must-have skills to about twelve. The more requirements you include, the less likely you are to attract people who are able to fill the role to your expectations. Focus on the crucial requirements. You can always add a "nice to have" section below the list of requirements.

#3: What challenges will my assistant face?

This question is important and also often overlooked. Your business has unique challenges. Your assistant might have the perfect experience and skills. However, he or she must also be able to produce quality work despite difficulties.

Challenges will stem from your management style. If you have a hands-off approach, you might offer sparse details or guidance on how a deliverable should be approached. Some people will need to ask clarifying questions or require detailed guidance, while others are self-directed and won't enjoy details outlined for them. Consider your management style as you create your requirements.

Other challenges might stem from your clients. If you work with executives, CEOs, doctors, or other highly educated or accomplished individuals, your client population could potentially have a higher number of direct, dominant, or demanding individuals. Your assistant might experience values violations if clients treat him or her as a subordinate or if clients are consistently demanding.

Consider the type of personality traits in an assistant that will work well with the population you serve. You can even use the "My Personality Traits" exercise in Chapter 2, but applied to an assistant instead of yourself.

ACTIVITY:

Write challenges specific to your management style, your clients, industry, environment, or other factors requiring specific skills or traits for your assistant to succeed.

_____

_____

_____

_____

_____

_____

_____

_____

If you feel overwhelmed by the many factors to consider as you shift from a solopreneur to having employees, try to prioritize and focus on first things first. Enjoy the process and resist the temptation to shortcut the steps to hire the perfect assistant for you. Preparation will save you headaches down the road. Remember, if you do not yet have a steady flow of clients, contract an assistant instead of hiring one.

Now, it's show-time! We've covered much ground to prepare you and your business. In "Part III: Coach!," we'll dive into a wide variety of topics you can employ to be a successful coach or consultant.

PART III: COACH!

—————— ☙ ——————

Coaching is a privilege and a responsibility. You partner with another person on a significant journey. Their journey. Your role is to ask good questions, tell targeted stories, synthesize what you hear, and, most of all, listen. You walk a delicate balance of objectivity and empathy. Often there's more than one perspective. But coaches must remember that first and foremost, it is NOT our journey. We are not the decision-maker. We are there to help clients make the best decisions for themselves.

Good coaches coach in an arena they know. What is your background? Where do you have considerable experience? That's where you should look for coaching opportunities. Why? Because you understand that world. We help people navigate delicate decisions. The more experience we have with the landscape where they work the better. This is where negative experiences we've had can be useful. It creates a shared understanding.

We will start section three with ethics.

17

CB

ETHICS

Kristin

What role does ethics play in coaching?

Ethics creates a standard of conduct to guide decision-making and behavior in situations a coach might face. Ethics guides us to tell the truth, keep our promises, and help someone within a respectful, trusting partnership.

A coach must work to the client's best interests and lack ego or judgmental interference.

Following are example ethical considerations:

Maintain a level of competence

As coaches, we owe it to our clients to keep our skills current to help our clients to the best of our ability. Competency can be honed through informal means such as reading and research, and more formal avenues such as certification, training, coursework or formal education.

Respect for the individual

Respect for individuality is expressed in many ways. One way is by valuing diversity and checking our biases about age, disability, gender, race, education level, socioeconomic status, and other demographics. This is not an exhaustive list and offers just a handful of examples.

Another way to show respect for the individual is not making assumptions or placing limitations on a person based on their assessment data. Assessments are instructive but are not always conclusive. In other words, an assessment might tell you one thing about a person that could lead you to believe he isn't capable of something. We must explore fully with a client and not jump to conclusions.

Acknowledge your limitations

When we are unqualified to handle a problem that surfaces during an engagement, we must be open and candid with clients that the problem is outside of our area of expertise, training, skill, or authority to address. Examples are mental health issues, financial problems, and legal concerns.

If you have credentials to serve clients in these areas, great! If you don't have the expertise, refer the individual to an expert or suggest they ask family and friends for recommendations.

Data handling and privacy

Not only is proper handling of data good practice, in many cases it's a legal requirement. If you live in Europe, General Data Protection Regulation (GDPR) applies in all member states to harmonize data privacy laws across Europe. The UK has the Information Commissioners Office who can fine individuals and companies for failure to meet GDPR rules.

Canada's GDPR equivalent is the Protection of Personal Information and Electronic Documents Act (PIPEDA). Research the data and privacy laws for your country to ensure you are compliant to avoid non-compliance penalties or fines.

In the U.S., data privacy and protection laws are less stringent than the GDPR. Regardless, sensitive handling of client data, respecting privacy, and preventing unauthorized access to information is an important ethical consideration when you've been entrusted with client data.

Take precautions to password protect your computer, do not share data with anyone that does not require access or has not been given permission by your client. Telling others who you are coaching is a privacy violation. Sharing details about the coaching is also a privacy violation.

I was once coaching two vice presidents in the same company. Sharing this fact with either person would be a breach of ethics as they were both looking to leave the organization. You could imagine the drama caused if I had loose lips about my clients.

Speak the truth

Avoid exaggerated claims about results you can bring. We can certainly share true stories of results clients have achieved, yet claims such as, "You will land your dream job in only two weeks," "I will help you increase your salary by 50 percent," or "You will lose 20 pounds in 20 days" should not be stated.

You can share true, data-backed statements like, "95 percent of my clients have received salary increases of at least 20 percent."

Conflicts of interest

Disclose any potential conflicts of interest to clients including, but not limited to, working with direct competitors, other contracts you have within the same organization, or compensation you receive if referring clients to other providers. It is understood, but I'll say it anyway, coaches should not engage in sexual or romantic relationships with a client or sponsor.

Confidentiality

Disclose no information without permission. Exceptions exist where permission is implicitly given. For example, if a job applicant completes an assessment as part of the application process, it's expected you will discuss the results with hiring decision-makers.

It would be inappropriate to share conversations or stories a client shared with you in confidence. Examples where information should *not* be kept confidential include illegal activity and imminent risk of danger to self or to others.

Reputable coaching certifications should address ethics as part of the curriculum. The consequences of ethics breaches could include loss of trust, reputational damage, loss of business, negative online reviews, contract termination, lawsuits or other legal action.

As a general rule, when working with a client, I obtain their permission before sharing anything. Even better, I suggest to clients that they, themselves, share information or data with a particular individual and why it would help them to share.

Following ethical guidelines is a non-negotiable practice for well-regarded coaches whom clients can confidently refer. And with client referrals comes discovery calls, so let's go there now!

18

☙

DISCOVERY CALLS
Kristin

When I began coaching, I made two big mistakes. I coached people during discovery calls, and I often let the duration of the call run beyond the scheduled time.

After I started certifying coaches, I learned other coaches were making the same mistake of coaching prospects in the discovery call. The purpose of a discovery call is to figure out if you are a fit to work together. Can you solve the customer's problem, and does she align with the profile you created of an *Ideal Client*?

Two main drivers cause coaches to begin coaching during discovery calls. The first one is being a natural helper. The second one is a need, even subconsciously, to prove our abilities to the prospect. You don't have to show the *how* when you can instead share brief stories of results you've achieved with clients who are in a comparable situation to the prospect.

Eventually, I learned to respect both my time and my prospective customer's time by using discovery calls for the intended purpose and not getting deep into the "how."

At the beginning of the call, outline the expectations: 10 minutes is reserved for the prospect to share her needs, and the remaining five minutes is to discuss outcomes she can expect to receive as well as to answer any questions she has. If discovery calls are longer, practice saying, *We have five minutes left. I want to make sure we cover* _____ .

When meeting with a prospect, jot down brief keywords he shares about his situation and the desired change or outcome he wants. Capturing his words allows you to create a powerful purpose statement in the proposal that will resonate more strongly than stock coaching jargon. You will also be able to tailor the services you put into the proposal based on the expressed needs of the client. See "Chapter 11: Proposals" for an example purpose statement.

At the beginning of the call, have a few questions ready to ask the prospect. Instead of asking him to explain the situation, keep him future-focused. One reason to use this approach is to prevent a lengthy historical dump of the client's problem. You want to keep him focused on what he wants to be better or different, rather than rehash his grievances.

Secondly, a future-focus will help you more clearly see how you can help, and it will bring to mind clients you've similarly helped. Here are a few example questions you might ask at the beginning of the call after you've explained the structure of the conversation:

If your goals were reached, what would that look like?

What is the number one thing you need help with?

What is your goal in working with a coach?

As you jot down phrases your potential client uses, choose a brief success story to share after he has finished speaking. You can segue into the story by saying something like, "You're looking to do x, y, and z. I can help you with that. Two months ago, I worked with a client in a comparable situation and he was able to [share the common goal your client achieved that the prospect desires]."

Adding data that emphasizes your success rate can also be helpful. Do you get results faster? Do you get your clients above average results?

For example:

"…landed an offer *in the first interview after we worked together.*"

"…received a *$25,000* annual salary increase."

"…landed a book deal *in two weeks.*"

"…received a promotion *60 days after our engagement* ended to an executive position *after two years of unsuccessful attempts* to be promoted."

Choose to share the story your client will most relate to. If an older person were experiencing ageism in hiring practices, I would choose to share a story of helping an older worker land a new position.

After you've shared a brief relatable story with your prospect, offer a high-level overview of what it will be like to work with you. Do you meet in person? How often? How long is the engagement? Give him an idea of what to expect without drilling into the details of *how*. No one wants to hear how the sausage is made. Instead, focus on the outcomes your client will receive.

If you haven't worked with paid clients, invite a few friends to go through your coaching in exchange for testimonials and accumulating stories for potential customers. Choose people who would benefit most from your program. You can offer a discounted rate or ask them to cover your out-of-pocket costs, such as assessments.

You can also share a brief story of your own experience to connect with the prospect, but be intentional to make the call about him, not you. Limit talking about yourself to a very brief story, if it is relevant.

Remember, your role as a coach is to think about how you can encourage a client and move him to action. Keep that in mind during prospect calls. The person should feel encouraged and confident you can help him move forward after talking with you.

Avoid making promises you can't guarantee, such as *you will land a job within two weeks,* or *your income will increase by 25 percent after working with me.* The client is responsible for taking action, and you can't take ownership for her actions. Instead, share stories of how you helped people and tangible outcomes you can guarantee, such as *you will have greater self-awareness to make more informed decisions.*

Finally, explain what will happen next. Will you be sending a formal proposal via email within 24 business hours? What will you do next? By when?

Two slight changes increased my prospects converting to paid clients. In a follow up, I gave prospective clients a one-page pdf of testimonials addressing problems I solved similar to their own. I also started offering three packages, such as Platinum, then Gold and Silver, with value increasing in each. As shared previously in the book, research shows people are more likely to buy when they have three options. Too many options yields the opposite effect – customers don't buy.

If a client is price conscious, consider counter-offering a scaled-down package if she says your proposal is out of her budget. For example, if she can't afford your full program, offer a mini version, such as a one-hour session instead of three sessions. You might still offer help. Some help is better than none.

For example, a resume writer could offer a resume critique service in addition to full-service resume writing services. Don't lower your price. It's unfair to clients who paid full price, and you undervalue yourself. Prices should change only if value is added or removed.

1. Outline call/Set expectations

2. Ask future-forward question such as, "What is your goal in working with a coach?"

3. Capture key words the prospect shares and his or her top goals

4. Share client success story with goals common to the prospect

5. Leave the prospect encouraged and confident you can help him or her move forward.

6. Provide a high-level view of your process (not the how)

7. Share the next steps

8. Follow up with a proposal

With all the new clients you'll be converting, now is the perfect time to launch into coaching process and best practices!

19

COACHING PROCESS & BEST PRACTICES
Judi

There are many diverse kinds of coaching. In this chapter we'll dig into coaching process and best practices that can be used across niches, and we'll also highlight and share some specific kinds of coaching such as leadership and intervention coaching to illustrate process and best practices.

Regardless of the coaching you deliver, or are thinking of delivering, you will find a treasure chest of techniques and tips in this chapter and also in the *Assessments & Tools* chapter that follows. You can incorporate these ideas into your existing process or use this chapter as a guide as you build out your process.

Before we get into the details of coaching, we want to share important thoughts on trust, as well as sympathy versus empathy. Throughout this book we've talked about the importance of trust. So trust is a fitting place for the coaching process and best practices chapter to begin.

Years ago, when I first started coaching, a CEO asked me to help two of his VPs. He told me their issue was fundamentally about trust, saying:

> "Neither of these people trusts the other, so the problems I've asked them to solve aren't getting addressed. The business is suffering because they lead large segments. Not only do they not trust each other, it's led to their teams not trusting each other. It has to be resolved."

His observation led me to research trust, and I narrowed it to five components and created a framework around it. Following is the result of that exercise, and I've used it successfully with thousands of people over the past 20 years.

To have trust in a person, I must believe five things:

1. S/he is *competent*. S/he can do what I want him/her to accomplish.
2. S/he is *reliable*. I can count on him/her. S/he won't let me down.
3. S/he is *fair*. I believe s/he will never take advantage of me.
4. S/he is *caring*. S/he has my best interests at heart.
5. S/he is *open*. We can talk about anything and I feel safe.

Here's what the framework looks like:

Competence and *reliability* are the "task" side of trust. This is about the ability to do the work.

Fairness and *caring* are the "relationship" side of trust. This is about collaborating well with people.

Openness is the bridge between building the relationship and doing the work. Openness gives a sense of safety and comfort. It creates a warm yet professional working environment.

When working on trust, think about how you will convey these five elements to potential clients and carry it through all the elements of your work together. Weave these components through your stories. Building a foundation of trust is non-negotiable.

SYMPATHY VS. EMPATHY

Remember the difference between sympathy and empathy. We need to understand what the person is going through; to step into their shoes and see their perspective. That's empathy. The pain we've experienced in our career helps with this. Every terrible experience you've had in your life and career is useful to you as a coach; it can supply necessary empathy. The worse it was for you, the better!

Every terrible experience you've had in your life and career is useful to you as a coach; it can supply necessary empathy.

I've experienced heartache as I worked in an organization going through massive change. People did not know if they would have their job in six months. I left because I just could no longer stand to see people crying in the hallways or the restroom.

I had a terrible separation from a business partner. Lawyers were involved. It turned my world upside down for 18 months. It was the worst anger I have ever experienced, mixed with guilt and regret. Guilt because I allowed it to happen, and regret because once upon a time we had so much fun together.

I've had humiliating performance evaluations.

A CEO raked me over the coals in a meeting with my boss (my boss got critical feedback, too!). When it was over, I asked my boss if he'd like to go somewhere with me and share a glass of arsenic!

I know what it feels like to bomb when you give an important presentation.

In hindsight, I am now grateful for these experiences. They have taught me empathy, humility, and compassion. They have also built my confidence...because I survived. I listened to the feedback and did something with it.

A CEO I worked with once told me my priorities were all wrong and he was really disappointed in my judgment. A few years later, he shook my hand and told me he was wrong when the local newspaper gave us unprecedented positive coverage after announcing the company was moving large numbers of jobs to another state.

We received two full pages in the business section highlighting our company history, best-selling products, and our philanthropy. My "priority" and "judgment" were to build a great relationship with that newspaper to highlight the good we did in the community.

Catalog all the dreadful experiences you've had. They can do the same for you. They also make wonderful stories you can use to help your clients. Even if you haven't experienced the exact situation as a client, your experiences will share common themes of loss, failure, disappointment, unexpected change, etc.

As for sympathy, you can feel empathy for your clients' experiences, but sympathy helps no one. You will carry it home with you and it will bloom into unhappiness. A coach listens to a lot of misery. Be empathetic, but know how to use that empathy to help. Sympathy will lead you to feel "sorry" for the person you are working with. If you don't see her as the strong, capable person she is, you will shortchange her.

In "Chapter 13: Niches," I mentioned three kinds of coaching: intervention, high potential, and high performance. I will detail below more about the process of these kinds of coaching.

INTERVENTION COACHING

Intervention coaching is a uniquely special type of coaching. This is where you work with people who have critical skills the organization or business needs but whom no one wants to work with. They are often described as cold, brusque, or prickly. And, of course, they don't realize it.

All my coaching engagements are voluntary. I will never coach someone who has been "mandated" to get coaching. It may start out that way, but I ask to meet with them one-on-one to get to know them and give them a chance to ask questions. Their perception of coaching is that it's *punishment* because they've been *bad*.

This first meeting lasts anywhere from 30 to 90 minutes. My approach with these people is always the same. I ask them to tell me what they enjoy about their work. Now this may seem odd since coaches may want to focus on the person first. But these people are often *task-oriented*. They feel far more comfortable focusing on work than on talking about themselves.

After I have listened carefully to all they have to say, I move on to asking what they are finding *frustrating* about their work. This is where they will really open up. Often I'm the only person who has asked them about this, and they sing to me like birds. They tell me *everything*. Then they're ready to talk about the interpersonal frustrations.

It's critical to let them get all this out. Be comfortable with silence if they pause. They find it to be more emotional than they were prepared for, and they need to regain their composure. Wait for them. Be gentle. Speak deliberately. At the end of an hour, which will feel quite intense to them, they will have experienced a sample coaching session. I ask them if they would like to continue with the coaching. I have never had a single person object to the coaching after this experience. They can't wait to get started.

One last and important point. If you want to do any type of corporate coaching – first line supervisors, middle or senior management – you need to think about how you will incorporate data into the project. Corporate people look for this. You'll need to learn a few psychometric tools and a 360 process. An appreciation for data and analysis on your part will add tremendous satisfaction to your work. We will share more about this topic in the next chapter, "Assessments & Tools."

HIGH POTENTIAL/HIGH PERFORMANCE EXECUTIVE COACHING

Executive coaching can be a natural pairing with group coaching. I fell into it. I was doing training with anywhere from 15 to 30 people per session. After a workshop, someone would come up to me and say something like, "This session was really interesting, and I'd like to talk to you about some of the things I realized going through it. Do you do any one-on-one work?" I can't believe when I think back to this that it took several of these interactions before I realized I was being asked to be their coach! Duh.

When starting a new coaching engagement, meet in advance with the person you will coach. Chances are you are a black box to him and he has no idea what's involved. Maybe he has heard horror stories about coaching or personally had an unpleasant experience.

Give him a chance to meet you and assess chemistry, which is critically important in a coaching relationship. You also get to explain what the coaching experience is like, how you work, and find out what the potential client needs help with. Your number one goal is to leave the meeting with him feeling comfortable moving forward with you and the sense that you can help him.

I make a point of explaining that my approach to executive coaching is to help people answer three questions:

Who am I?

We spend more time trying to figure out other people than trying to figure out ourselves!

What's important to me (values)?

A life that is not lived according to your values is not a life worth living and many problems arise when we aren't living our values.

What do I want, and what do I need to be effective?

These are two vastly different things. What we want are our aspirations. What we need are the things we lack that *keep us from our aspirations*. These are things we may need to learn or we may need others to supply for us.

I also let the client know several other important things. First, this is *his* project, not mine. I'm an ally, an advocate, a partner and, sometimes, a facilitator. All decisions are his. Second, my job is not to fix or change him. He will decide what he wants to do better or differently. Third, I will offer my opinion or advice if asked. But mostly I will tell him stories that will help him to decide.

Next, hold an expectations meeting with the coachee

and his supervisor. In this meeting, you do three things:

1. Ask the supervisor why she felt coaching would be valuable for the person. Then, ask her to list the person's strengths. Take notes. You will need these notes for the proposal. I can't tell you how often the person I coach will tell me later that this was the first time his supervisor told him many of these things! He hadn't even received the feedback in a performance evaluation.

   Next, ask the coachee if there is anything he would add to the list of strengths. Often he is so amazed to hear the supervisor's list, he doesn't add anything.

2. Ask the coachee what he wants to gain from coaching. The way I phrase it is to ask, "Imagine it's a year from now, and you've worked with me that whole time. What will you have then that you don't have now?" He tells me what he wants to get and I take notes.

3. Ask the supervisor if there is anything she would add to the list. It's rarely more than one thing, if anything.

Now you have the basic information for your proposal. I have a preference – because I have two decades of experience inside a company – for shaping a proposal into three sections:

Purpose: why is this person being coached?
Process: what will the work look like?
Fees: Professional services fee and what it includes.

You can see a sample coaching proposal in "Chapter 11:

Proposals." I always divide the work into phases. Each phase of my coaching process has between four and five 60–90-minute sessions. Yours will vary.

Phase one centers around self-awareness. This is where I use my psychometric tools. I have favorites, but my toolkit has at least half a dozen, depending on what the client needs. I also include a 360 in this phase – a performance evaluation tool that asks for feedback about an employee from all directions: their managers, coworkers, and direct reports. The 360 is usually a questionnaire given to people chosen by the coachee and their supervisor.

Phase two is about understanding others. In this phase, I use results of the 360 to help the person decide where he wants to focus, using a development plan. Then we begin that work.

Phase three is geared to helping him lead his team, and I often include a workshop. Between phase one and phase two, we have a process check meeting with the supervisor. At this meeting, I talk about the number of sessions we've had and might review the tools we've used.

In many of my assignments, I've also coached the supervisor, and I use this as an opportunity to do "paired comparisons" where they learn what they have in *common* with each other and where they are *different*. This is especially important if there is tension or conflict between them.

Between phase two and phase three we have another process check meeting. Here we will discuss highlights of the 360, what the coachee has decided to focus on, and what help or support he might need from the supervisor.

When the coaching is complete, we have a wrap up meeting. This is essentially my report card. We revisit the purpose of the coaching. Did the coachee get all the things he mentioned in the expectations meeting? Virtually all the time, clients report getting all those things and more than they initially realized.

My engagements now are quite long, so I include three check-in meetings that will carry us another six months beyond the end of the coaching. The first is thirty days after coaching is complete. Then sixty days after that, a second check-in meeting is held. Finally, three months after the second check-in, we have the final meeting.

This means, on average, I work with an executive for 18 months. By now we have a really solid relationship, and this is where so many of my future engagements come from. People I have coached regularly come to me to coach a co-worker.

Another outcome of this approach is the leader will want me to start working with members of his or her team and then work with the entire group through group coaching to increase effectiveness of the entire department.

These are the engagements that mean so much to me. I have relationships that span decades with people I just love to be with. And they regularly bring me more projects.

Coach Reminders

This is their project, not ours.

We are an ally, advocate, partner, or facilitator.

All decisions are theirs.

Our job is not to fix or change them.

Clients decide what they want to do better or differently.

We can offer our opinion or advice if asked.

Mostly we will tell stories to help them decide.

The Coaching Process

Contracting
- Discuss and set expectations for the engagement (yours, coachee, and his or her supervisor)

Planning – elements of the engagement
- Preliminary design by the coach based on expectations
- Check for agreement

Conversation/live action – a blend of tools and process
- Ask questions
- Listen
- Reframe
- Ask more questions
- Support the exploration with exercises and assessments

Debriefing
- Check for understanding
- Reinforce insights/awareness
- Decide next steps

Periodic process checks
- What have you learned? (insights and observations)
- How have you used it? (practical applications)
- What has been the result? (What's better? What still needs attention? What help do you need?)

Wrap up meeting
- What's the overall result of the coaching?
- Were the goals met?
- What's needed to continue personal development and growth?

Ongoing support
- Check-ins or "tune ups" (optional)
- Periodic meetings to continue growth

These coaching techniques can be adapted to your specific niche or help you determine your best process.

In this chapter, I recommended using tools as part of your coaching process based on the needs of your client. In the next chapter, "Assessments & Tools," I cover a variety of assessments, frameworks, and effective coaching questions. At the end of the chapter, Kristin will guide you to build or enhance your own coaching process using these tools.

20

CB

ASSESSMENTS & TOOLS
Judi

COACHING ASSESSMENTS

Assessments can add tremendous value to the client and your business. Several thousand different assessments are available. They range from simple questionnaires available for free on the internet to scientifically-based, reliable and valid tools that require certification.

For some of these tools, you are only eligible for certification with an undergraduate or master's degree in the humanities (usually psychology) and/or specific training. If you want to work with large corporations or organizations, this is practically a must.

Expertise with assessments automatically propels your status in the coaching world. Corporate people work with data and expect it from all types of vendors and suppliers. We've covered using assessments for yourself in previous chapters. You can use what you learn from those to see how you are similar or different from your clients. Using assessments with clients also adds value to you and your business in multiple ways:

1. *Better understanding of who you are working with.* Use the data from the assessments to understand your client better. It is a powerful window into what's important to them and how to work with them.

2. *Find the underlying cause of issues faster.* Showing people their data unleashes a torrent of awareness. You are there to ask questions and guide their insight.

3. *Additional expertise.* Some of the marketers of assessments may allow you to become a "trainer" and certify other people.

4. *Additional income.* You pay one rate and charge the client another. Your markup might be anywhere from 20 – 50 percent. That's a fantastic way to add to your margins. Most of the executive and business coaches I know use assessments. This is a classic mix of Pig (coaching) and Chicken (assessments). See "Chapter 7: Starting a Business" for a complete explanation of Chicken and Pig businesses, and why we recommend them.

Talk to coaches who use assessments. Which ones do they like best? Which ones do their clients like best? Which are easiest to use? Where did they start? What did they use first?

Following are some of our favorite assessments.

CliftonStrengths® – an assessment created by the Gallup Organization and also the starting point of YouMap® (more about YouMap® later). CliftonStrengths is wonderful for people who have never experienced a psychometric tool. Who doesn't want to hear about their top natural talents? CliftonStrengths is a safe starting point because it focuses on what's right with people.

Following is a sample of the full 34 strengths. The top five assessment is less expensive and quite effective for coaching. However, if a person is struggling, the full 34 can often reveal why. A certification is available, but not required, for administering CliftonStrengths.

STRENGTHEN

1.	**Achiever**
2.	**Responsibility**
3.	**Intellection**
4.	**Input**
5.	**Positivity**
6.	Woo
7.	Activator
8.	Communication
9.	Relator
10.	Arranger

NAVIGATE

11.	Individualization
12.	Focus
13.	Futuristic
14.	Strategic
15.	Learner
16.	Includer
17.	Empathy
18.	Connectedness
19.	Harmony
20.	Significance
21.	Ideation
22.	Maximizer
23.	Belief
24.	Self-Assurance
25.	Command
26.	Analytical
27.	Competition
28.	Discipline
29.	Consistency
30.	Adaptability
31.	Developer
32.	Context
33.	Restorative
34.	Deliberative

You lead with **Executing** CliftonStrengths themes.

■ **EXECUTING** themes help you make things happen.

■ **INFLUENCING** themes help you take charge, speak up and make sure others are heard.

■ **RELATIONSHIP BUILDING** themes help you build strong relationships that hold a team together.

■ **STRATEGIC THINKING** themes help you absorb and analyze information that informs better decisions.

READ "IDENTIFY YOUR UNIQUE CONTRIBUTION: THE CLIFTONSTRENGTHS DOMAINS" SECTION TO LEARN MORE ›

Strengths Insight Guide, © Gallup®

DiSC® – a behavioral tool by Wiley that describes four kinds of behavior – *Dominance, Influence, Steadiness* and *Conscientiousness*. Useful for team building, communication, and conflict management, DiSC® requires certification.

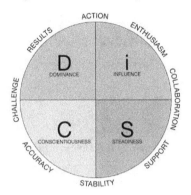

DiSC® Work of Leaders – highlights a leader's priorities, behaviors, and top leadership strengths and challenges.

DiSC® Work of Leaders DiSC, © John Wiley & Sons, Inc.

WorkPlace Big Five Profile™ – a tool created by Paradigm Personality Labs with forty years of research to back it up. Participants learn their natural personality traits and the kinds of activities they enjoy and that energize them.

This tool is great for team building, conflict management, and individual self-discovery at any level. Certification is required to administer this assessment tool.

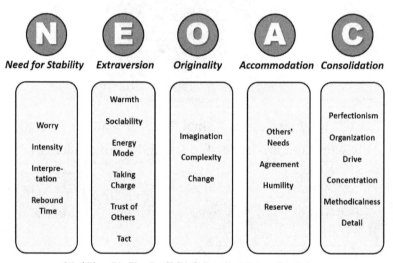

WorkPlace Big Five Profile™, © *Paradigm Personality Labs*

Thinking Styles – an assessment that reveals how people gather information and use it to make decisions. I use this for executive coaching to help leaders understand how they make decisions.

Making good decisions, solving problems, and clearly seeing opportunities are all outcomes of effective thinking. Good thinking is empowering – it builds confidence and demonstrates strong leadership.

Thinking Styles, © *NCS Pearson, Inc.*

YouMap® – reveals a person's *strengths, values, preferred skills* and *personality-based interests.*

Its beauty is two-fold. First, it's simple and easy to understand. People get it right away. Second, it's highly effective and useful across a wide range of situations from student coaching, career coaching, succession planning, talent acquisition, professional development, team building, executive coaching, life coaching, military transition, personal branding, and more. A certification is available, but not required, to access YouMap®.

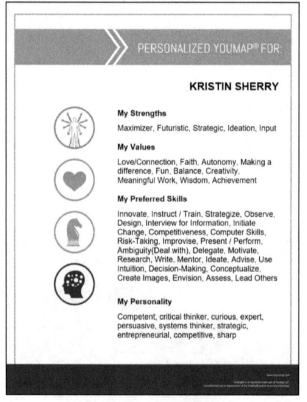

YouMap®, © YouMap LLC

YouMap® Background

Kristin: I was first certified as both a career and executive coach through an employer beginning in 2007. Over the years, I chose to complete a half dozen certifications for various assessment tools and also used a few tools that didn't require certification.

I always felt like I was piecing and patching together information to create a holistic view of my direct reports and, later, my clients. As it turns out, other practitioners felt the same way when I posed questions in various coaching groups. When I couldn't find a tool that displayed a simple, yet robust, view of clients, I decided to build what I needed.

After speaking with approximately 2,000 people and analyzing the data, a clear pattern emerged. Four consistent themes contributed to a person's fit and satisfaction in a role: strengths, values, preferred skills, and personality-based interests.

After working with a lot of people to bring YouMap® to life, then testing and piloting, I started to have immediate success with clients. I was approached by a woman who worked in Human Resources who wanted me to train her to use the tool. I knew the assessment was getting my clients results, but was it the chef or the ingredients? I needed to know the answer.

In 2017, I applied for the YouMap® trademark, though it was years in the making. Today, coaches worldwide use YouMap® for leadership coaching, job seekers, grief counseling, career transition, communication consulting, talent acquisition, and more. They are uncovering their clients' strengths, values, skills, and personality and experiencing similar transformational results. In 2020, YouMap® received the Career Innovator Award from Career Directors International. I was relieved it was the ingredients not the chef.

COACHING TOOLS

Years ago, I took part in TQM training at the company where I worked. Total Quality Management has some great tools that can easily be incorporated into coaching. For example, following are some of the questions I use over and over.

THE FIVE QUESTIONS

A tool to help leaders strategically prioritize to get better results is the Five Questions.

The Five Questions, when used internally and externally, can give an individual, group, department/ division or entire organization a broad range of information that can be quickly distilled into the "critical few." Your clients will know what to use, what to correct, what the barriers are, how others are willing to engage or provide resources, and where to start.

Decide the focus. What or who are you asking about? It can be about *yourself*, it can be about *another person*, it can be about a *team*, it can be about a *project*, and it can be about *your business* as a whole.

Grab a pen and paper, or fire up a document on your computer, to capture your thoughts as you step through this clarifying exercise.

QUESTION #1:
WHAT'S WORKING?

This question is designed to reveal the benefits and positives of whatever you are examining. How can these be used or expanded?

QUESTION #2:
WHAT NEEDS TO BE DONE BETTER, DIFFERENTLY, OR MORE OF

This question introduces the need for change in a non-threatening way that opens people to possibilities. It is future-focused. By looking across the suggestions, begin to think about what the proposed changes have in common so that they can be grouped and then focused on the critical few changes.

QUESTION #3:
WHAT'S PREVENTING IMPROVEMENT?

This question is designed to uncover barriers. Again, look at what the barriers may have in common, focusing on the critical few. This is also a suitable time to ask about obstacles that might impede progress on the things that need to be done better or differently.

QUESTION #4:

IF YOU COULD MAKE ONE CHANGE,

WHAT WOULD IT BE?

This question can bring to light the most important change that needs to be made. Is this the best place to start?

QUESTION #5:

HOW COULD YOU HELP AND

WHAT HELP DO YOU NEED?

By asking yourself, and others, how you/they might help can accomplish two things:

1. You, or they, may recognize that you, or they, are barriers to the improvement and something about your or their behavior or attitude needs to change.
2. You can develop a resource inventory based on skills, talent, knowledge, experience, etc. in the group to staff projects.

FIVE USES FOR THE FIVE QUESTIONS

These questions work in lots of situations. Following are five examples, but the uses are almost endless.

1. When you start working in a new position, ask the Five Questions of your boss, peers, direct reports, other departments, and anyone who is willing to answer. They will help you to understand others'

beliefs so you can set your goals and manage your priorities.

2. Conduct focus groups with external and internal customers to increase customer satisfaction. One thought: You may want to remove Question #5 when conducting a focus group with external customers. However, you should definitely include it with internal customers – you never know how much they might be willing to help.

3. Create an employee survey using the Five Questions to identify employees' perceptions, likes, dislikes, and priorities for your work environment.

4. Use the Five Questions as a basis for an employee coaching session or performance review. Asking employees the Five Questions about their work and on-the-job behavior helps them to find their own strengths and areas for improvement.

5. Send the Five Questions to a group when they are invited to a planning session. If they think about their responses prior to the session, the discussion will be more constructive and collaborative.

1. *What's working?*
2. *What needs to be done better, differently, or more of?*
3. *What's preventing improvement?*
4. *If you could make one change, what would it be?*
5. *How can you help and what help do you need?*

FIVE USES FOR THE FIVE QUESTIONS

1. *When you, or someone else, is starting a new role*
2. *Customer focus groups*
3. *Employee surveys*
4. *Coaching session or performance review*
5. *Planning Group*

PLUS/DELTA EVALUATION

The Plus/Delta is a quick tool to evaluate anything. It is designed to collect information about what participants find beneficial (+) and what they would change (Δ). You can evaluate a meeting, product, process, document, department, team, or even a person. Following is a visual of the tool.

+	**Δ**
What's working/ went well	What needs to be done better, differently, more?

Process

1. You can use the tool as a handout or draw the illustration onto flip chart paper or a white board. The following exercise works well with up to eight people. For larger groups, break them down into groups of six to eight people.

2. Start with the left-hand side. Ask people to list what's working or what they like about whatever you are focusing on. You might ask for a brief list, say three to five things. The idea is to start a discussion. In the right-hand column, list all the things that need to be done better, differently, or more of. In other words, what changes would bring a better chance of success.

   For example:

   a. What did you like about today's meeting? (+)
      What would you change for the next meeting? (Δ)
   b. What do you like about that product? (+)
      What could we change to make it better? (Δ)
   c. What do you like about working with our team? (+) What could we do better, differently or more of to be more effective? (Δ)
   d. What does your supervisor do well? (+)
      What could s/he do better, differently, or more of to be more effective? (Δ)
   e. What is going well in our organization? (+)
      What do we need to do better, differently, or more of to achieve our vision (or reach certain goals)? (Δ)

3. When you have all the information, find the "critical few" on the delta side. For example, give each person five votes to apply to the list. They can put up to two votes on any one item. See what most people choose. What are the top two or three items? What is the most important item to do first? Or see if the list naturally lends itself to what needs to be done first.

   Note: Ask each group to organize their lists into types of improvements (e.g. process, culture, profitability, etc.). Then, bring the groups together, review the lists, combine again if needed, and finally ask participants to vote, looking across the group lists.

4. You have the beginning of a plan, or at least a data-driven request.

5. For large initiatives, create a team or teams to tackle the items and repeat the plus/delta exercise for each selected item.

6. Make sure to summarize the suggestions at the end of the meeting! You can send the summary to anyone who needs to receive it.

Other uses for the Plus/Delta

- An individual's performance
- An individual's readiness for a promotion or project
- Business forms or documents
- Training workshops
- Standard operating procedures
- A system or workflow
- New ideas of any kind

- Customer service levels
- Facilities design
- The lunch menu
- In short, anything that needs to be better!

EFFECTIVE QUESTIONS

The purpose of Effective Questions is to focus on what's already working, which is energizing and supportive. These questions then clarify objectives to create a clear target or goal. Lastly, they create agreement for the next steps and turn "forcing" into collaborating. These three specific questions that begin with *tell me about*, *why*, and *how*, come from *Enlightened Leadership* by Ed Oakley and Doug Krug.[13]

These questions help a person solve problems and are highly effective to use with direct reports to build confidence and initiative.

The Process

Effective questions move people forward. To ensure you understand the issue, you might start with...

"Tell me about..."

> Tell me about what has been happening.
>
> Tell me about the situation.
>
> Tell me about your frustrations.

This is an open-ended question that really helps you to understand what the other person is thinking and feeling. You will learn what energizes him, what frightens him, what he wants. This is your "research" question whenever you need more insight about an issue or a situation.

When you have a good understanding of the situation, you can switch into the goal-oriented questions of *What*. For example, ask:

What do you want to accomplish?

What will you need?

What might be a problem?

What do you think about the project so far?

What's working?

What needs to be done better or differently?

What's preventing the improvements?

What are the most important things you must do to make this happen?

What kind of support do you need to get those results?

When there is agreement around the goal, shift into the action-oriented questions, the *How*:

How do you think you could do it?

How soon do you want to start?

How long do you think it will take?, etc.

By the end of these questions, the person has a sense of how he can create his own success. You become the facilitator, mentor, coach.

What are the benefits of this approach? Imagine your colleagues with a three-by-five card on their forehead. The card reads *Tell me about...*, *What and How...* You can put this beginning on almost any thought to turn it into an Effective Question.

EFFECTIVE QUESTIONS FOCUS ON

What's already working – they are energizing and supportive.

Clarifying the objectives – they create a clear target or goal.

Agreement for the next steps – they turn "forcing" into collaborating.

AGREEMENT BUILDING QUESTIONS

Before leaving a discussion or meeting, wouldn't it be nice if all participants knew everyone was on the same page, everyone agreed to what was decided, and everyone knew the next steps? Agreement Building Questions give all parties involved in a conversation the information necessary to build accountability and foster consistency of message. They also help make sure the individuals impacted receive communication about decisions and actions, even if they weren't part of the discussion.

The Process

At the end of a meeting, or when changing to a new topic or agenda item, go through these questions to ensure all participants understand what is expected and agree to the messaging. Be sure to record the answers.

What did we decide today?

This question helps to make sure that everyone is in complete agreement with the decisions that were made.

Who is going to do what? By when?

These questions help to make sure that there is certainty around next steps and that a framework for accountability is set up.

Who needs to know about this?

This question ensures that everyone will be in the loop and no one will be left out, even those who aren't part of the meeting or discussion. This is a critical question for improving communication and confidence in one another.

What is the message and the tone of that message?

What do you want people to think and feel when they hear the message? This question makes sure that everyone is on the same page and that all the people involved communicate with one voice.

You can use these questions in your coaching practice at the end of a session to build accountability with clients. Also guide clients to use them to build their effectiveness at work or even in their personal lives.

AGREEMENT BUILDING QUESTIONS

1. *What did we decide today?*
2. *Who is going to do what? By when?*
3. *Who needs to know about this?*

---

4. What is the message and the tone of that message?

Modify these questions to work best with your coaching. For example, you might only need the first two or three questions.

STRATEGIC COMMUNICATION MODEL

If communication is part of your coaching, the Strategic Communication Model is a useful tool. You can use this model in your own business and coach your clients with it.

The Process

Think about what you communicate to other people and what you search for when others communicate with you. Imagine you work in a building with four floors. Each floor focuses on a specific type of communication, shown here.

NOW WHAT?
(4TH FLOOR)

SO WHAT?
(3RD FLOOR)

INFORMATION
(2ND FLOOR)

DATA
(1ST FLOOR)

As you read each type of communication on the four floors of the building, ask yourself:

1. Where do I spend the most time?
2. Am I preoccupied with just getting the *facts*?
3. Do I put facts into context to give me *information*?
4. Do I use information to seek *knowledge* about a particular issue or situation?
5. Do I take time to discuss with others not only the implications of the situation but a good *understanding* of what to do? (Using tools and a process really helps!)

THE 1ST FLOOR

People on this floor talk about *facts* and *data*. For example:

"Revenue this month was $4,000 dollars."

They may see themselves as someone who is just responsible for passing along a fact without any further responsibility.

THE 2ND FLOOR

People on this floor talk about *information*. They put facts and data into context. For example:

"Revenue this month was $4,000, but I had projected monthly revenue of $6,000. I have a shortfall."

Floors 1 and 2 deal mostly with *what*. People who are on this floor may wonder about their role in what they've learned, a key step in taking responsibility for the information that's delivered and received.

THE 3RD FLOOR

People on this floor seek *knowledge*. For example:

"I had a $2,000 monthly shortfall which jeopardizes launching a new course system. Without that system, several other projects will be delayed and passive income goals will not be met. What caused this shortfall and what am I going to do about it?"

They think about the impact of what's communicated. Now it's about "*So what?*" People on this floor feel a keen sense of responsibility and accountability for communication, what they send out and what they receive. They are engaged.

THE 4TH FLOOR

People on this floor seek *understanding*. They are tuned to their environment (external as well as internal) and are always seeking to understand not only the impact of what is happening in their world, but what they can do about it. For example:

"Financial concerns are delaying an important project. We need to do three things: find out what is causing the revenue shortfall and what to do about it, look at ways we can minimize the impact of the shortfall (e.g. where can we cut costs until revenue is back on track), and finally, how do we reorganize our priorities and ensure everyone is on board so that overall goals are met? What do we need to do to ensure this doesn't happen again?"

They listen for and talk about the *"Now what?"* These people are *leaders who actively lead.* Continuously looking to understand your internal and external environment over time develops *wisdom* about the world you work in. Wise people thrive and so do their worlds.

Observe

On which of the four floors do you spend most of your time? You should be able to navigate all the floors, however, where is your time best used?

What do you ask about, what do you hear, what do you tell others, how do you contribute? Use *The Five Questions* (introduced at the beginning of this "Coaching Tools" section) to help you, or your clients, spend the maximum time on the top (4th) floor. Thousands of clients have told us these tools help build wisdom.

Next Steps

When planning a presentation, speaking to prospects, creating social media content or other marketing efforts, think about the amount of time you want to spend on each "floor."

Twenty percent may be enough on the first two floors, with 40 percent spent on the 3rd floor to ensure adequate knowledge for your intended audience, and the balance of

40 percent on the top floor using understanding to make decisions and act.

Modify this basic approach based on your understanding of your audience and their needs.

The Four Levels of Communication:

Now what?

So what?

Information

Data

ADDITIONAL TOOLS & COACHING QUESTIONS

Gary Chapman is a marriage counselor who took his notes from decades of sessions and created the popular *Five Love Languages* book and companion process. The *Five Love Languages* is great for personal coaching and can be adapted for corporate work in terms of recognition. The love languages are *Words of Affirmation, Acts of Service, Quality Time, Receiving Gifts*, and *Appropriate Physical Touch*.

The Passion Test by Janet Bray Attwood and Chris Attwood. This process helps you name what's most important to you. I got certified in the process in 2008 – almost 15 years ago. What I learned still holds true for me today, and I use it to keep my passions strong:

- Spending quality time with Wayne, my husband of 57 years

- Living a peaceful, serene, joyful life
- Living in a beautiful home surrounded by nature
- Working as part of dynamic teams
- Building thriving businesses with impact

Develop three to five criteria for each of your passions and then measure on a scale of 1 – 5 how much of the passion you have in your life. You can develop criteria for each passion. For example, regarding spending quality time with my husband, we take annual trips together, we eat dinner together a minimum of four nights weekly, we spend weekends together doing something we both enjoy. When I'm traveling, we speak on the phone twice daily. Focus on your passions with the lowest scores to build them to where they need to be.

In addition to the coaching frameworks we've shared, following are some other effective coaching questions.

What's the most important thing we need to talk about today?

I learned this question from reading Susan Scott's book *Fierce Conversations*. This question can quickly take you to what needs to be talked about, the important and the urgent.

Evaluate your client's learning with this question:

What's new since I saw you last?

This question gives insight into two things – 1) anything critical that has happened since the last meeting and its impact, and 2) whether she is using anything she learned from the last meeting and the results.

The key to effective coaching is asking better questions. Following is one final list of questions to try with clients.

What's missing in your life right now?

What do you most want to achieve as your top priority?

If you could start over, what would you do differently?

What is in your control to change?

Who do you respect and would s/he handle the situation?

What have you tried so far?

What action can you take now?

What is a first step you will take? By when?

What's the cost of not taking action?

What's the benefit of not taking action?

What will change if you achieve your goal?

How will you know if you've succeeded?

Who do you have to support you?

How will you hold yourself accountable?

What have you learned?

Who was the best leader/manager you've ever had?

Who was your worst/most disappointing leader/manager?

Kristin: You can use the resources in this chapter to build, or add to, your coaching process. For example, if you are a life coach, you could do something like the following:

#1: Try Starting with The Five Questions

What's working?

What needs to be done better, differently, or more of?

What's preventing improvement?

If you could make one change, what would it be?

How can you help and what help do you need?

#2: Guide and Assess Based on Responses

Once you have answers to these five questions, you'll understand what is going well. This allows you to encourage your client to pursue more of the things that are going well in her life. You will also know her barriers and most needed change from questions three and four. As you hear the client's thoughts on what needs to be better or different, you can choose the best tools to use.

For example, if she is struggling the most with confidence, YouMap® is known for increasing self-confidence because it focuses on what's right with people. The profile also has a companion workbook full of activities and questions you can use in your sessions.

If the client is experiencing conflict, you could take her through an assessment such as DiSC® Productive Conflict. Another alternative could be an Emotional Intelligence (EQ) questionnaire or assessment. Conflict often stems from EQ issues. The only EQ assessment I'm familiar with is EQi2, which assesses five dimensions: stress management, decision making, self-perception, interpersonal, and self-expression. There are free EQ assessments online, but I can't vouch for them. Test drive a few before using them with clients.

#3: Try the Plus/Delta

Each time you meet with your client, you can use the Plus/Delta tool combined with some questions we included in the chapter. For example:

> *What's going well?*
> *What would you like to change?*
> *What's the most important thing we need to talk about today?*

#4: Build Action into the Process

After each session, give your client some form of "homework" to build new skills and work toward a goal.

#5: Build Accountability into the Process

Build accountability into your process with agreement-building questions such as, "What are you committing to do? By when? What help do you need?" Guide your client to set realistic goals in her scope of control. You should also build accountability into the coaching by starting each session with a celebration of a goal completed from the previous week.

#6: Experiment and Hone the Process

Honing means experimenting. When I started coaching, I would test drive tools with employees, friends, and in my volunteer work. In time, I found tools I preferred, questions that were impactful, and a process that worked for clients.

Don't use tools for the sake of it. Everything starts with a client goal. Draw from your toolkit based on what a client needs to meet a stated goal. I like *"Tell me about," "What," and "How"* questions to elicit goals and actions.

Tell me about what's happening with your manager.
What would you like to see happen? (goal-focused)
How might you make that happen? (action-focused)

Regardless of the kind of coaching you do, the example I just shared should be enough to get you started on creating a process, or enhancing the process you currently have. Now, if you've decided to focus on group coaching, or offer a hybrid group and individual coaching program, the process is a little different. Let's talk about that next.

21

CƷ

GROUP COACHING
Judi

People have three basic needs:

They want to be heard.

They want to be understood.

They want to belong.

This is the foundation of group coaching. Everything else is just the bells and whistles you choose to add.

Lots of things have contributed to the fragmentation of society over the last 50 years, and because I've been around a long time (I'm 76 as of this writing), I've lived through them. Most recently, people talk about "technology" as the culprit because so many people live on their cell phones. I am no exception. My husband often complains that his chief competition is my laptop because it goes everywhere with me, and my face is always in it.

Bowling Alone, a book I read over 20 years ago, laid out a similar story about society disintegrating through the lens of the dramatic drop in bowling leagues! In any event, human beings yearn for connection, to know that we are not alone, despite all the time we spend doing things alone!

Group coaching directly addresses this need for connection *plus* learning. How you choose to put a group together is up to you. The kinds of group coaching are infinite but tend to fall into the categories of topic-based (such as fitness or career), mission-based (a common mission of the group such as cleaning up your community), business growth (how to expand or grow a business), or goal and accountability-based (members keep each other accountable and focused on goal attainment).

For example, AA and Gamblers Anonymous offer group coaching for people dealing with addiction. They are topic-based and accountability-based. They've been around a long time. AA's spin-off, Al-Anon, provides group coaching for people who live with or care about someone with an addiction, which could be seen as topic-based and mission-based.

Here are some basics around group coaching:

Central theme or opportunity

Why will these people come together? They are interested in learning as well as having connection. What do they want to learn?

Target market

What will these people have in common? What kind of journey are they interested in?

Common interests

What content will you supply to engage them, create a path for them, give them a sense of fulfillment and accomplishment?

Common goals

What do they want to have at the end or what do they want to build?

Incidentally, your group coaching practice does not have to end. I know people who have taken part in a business group coaching program called *Vistage* that have been members for years. I was in a chapter dedicated to coaches and consultants.

Vistage, originally known as TEC, is the other end of the spectrum from AA, Al-Anon and Gamblers Anonymous. This is group coaching on steroids, focused on business. TEC started in 1957 when a Wisconsin businessman named Robert Nourse met with four fellow chief executives in the office of the Milwaukee Valve Company. His aim was to test a simple, yet revolutionary idea. He wanted them to share their knowledge and experiences to help each other generate better results for themselves and their businesses. Soon this group of businessmen were probing, asking questions and making suggestions. They challenged each other, working together to solve issues and grow.

Today, *Vistage* operates in twenty countries around the world. Members meet in private advisory groups every month under the same guiding principles—to help one another become better leaders, make better decisions, and achieve better results. What's more, *Vistage* and its affiliate members are connecting in ways Robert never could have imagined: learning from hundreds of top industry speakers, tapping into a vast online resource library, and collaborating around the world.

Vistage has become a large organization with the equivalent of "corporate headquarters" and facilitators who lead and manage the individual chapters. If you are an experienced coach, you can apply to become a *Vistage* chair which combines individual coaching sessions with your members and the monthly meetings which you facilitate.

On a smaller scale, my first group coaching project was given to me by someone who had started a group called TEAF (The Executive Assistant Forum). She was moving across the country and could no longer lead the group (years before Zoom!). Her husband was a TEC chair, so she had started a group for all the secretaries who worked for the TEC CEO members – eight of them.

It was wildly successful. We met monthly. I treated them like junior CEOs because, as I explained to them, their job was to manage a person who managed a business. They learned, grew, and became better administrators just as their bosses were learning to become better CEOs.

So what's in between these two extremes? A lot! I created a group coaching product called *Aspiring Executives*. We had between eight and twelve people per program, and the sessions took place over several months. Here's what some of the sessions can look like:

Welcome session – getting to know each other, why are you here, what do you want to learn.

CliftonStrengths assessment – begin the learning journey. Who doesn't want to learn about their gifts? Many YouMap® coaches have also found success using the YouMap® profile as a group coaching tool, which incorporates CliftonStrengths.

Creating a Great Workplace – learning about and discussing what an effective workplace looks like.

Communication and behavioral styles – DiSC® is a great resource to guide conversations on communication and behavior.

Leadership – vision, getting buy-in around the vision followed by successful execution. DiSC Work of Leaders® can take them through this.

Managing – understanding various human traits and the abilities that accompany them – WorkPlace Big Five Profile™ from Paradigm Personality Labs can fill the bill here.

360 feedback – targeting what they need to boost their effectiveness and hearing what people already appreciate about them – their strengths and skills.

In between the group coaching sessions I conducted, which lasted half a day or a full day, they had one-on-one coaching conversations. We've targeted, honed and strengthened our group coaching processes so that they are flexible for a variety of needs and audiences. Sometimes they are as quick as two hours for people who just can't be away from their work for a full or half day.

What all group coaching has in common is:

1. **An opening where members talk about how they are doing** – "How was your week?" or "How was your month?" – whatever amount of time since they were together last. The beauty of this is the amount of sharing and caring that occurs. Members develop bonds and learn from one another. It also puts them in the right frame of mind for the session. If this were a dinner, this would be like enjoying an appetizer. This opening often lasts an hour or more of a half-day session and sometimes ninety minutes for a full day session. The idea is for everyone to share – the good, the bad, the ugly and then process it as a group. In my experience, the impact is astounding.

2. **An assessment or framework** – the main course. Each assessment measures something different so choose an assessment based on what you want to assess in the group. Spend a good amount of time on this section, ensuring they understand the feedback and how it fits with their issues and their world. Then they can learn from it and get specific ideas of what to do with it. Encourage them to share with the

others, strengthening the group's bond through empathy and support.

3. **A tool or process** – something that will help an aspect of their work – doing a talent assessment, giving feedback, a coaching process they can use with people who report to them. Think of the tool or process as a follow-up skill-builder that benefits the group based on what was revealed in the previous step. For example, do many members of the group struggle with effectively giving feedback to direct reports? *This step puts action to assessment results.*

4. **Wrap up** – what did you get out of today? What are you going to use? This carries over into their one-on-one coaching sessions and is a perfect place to start the discussion. Did you do what you said you were going to do? How did it go? This creates accountability.

5. **Evaluation** – my favorite tool is the plus/delta. What did you like? What could we have done better, differently, more of? We have included plus/delta in "Chapter 20: Assessments & Tools." It has a wide range of uses. Visit rvrhodesinc.com for more on group coaching.

MASTERMINDS

Kristin: Masterminds are another form of group coaching where you bring people together to learn from and support each other. Often they are peers, and this format helps them build their business.

A straightforward way to start setting up such a group is to talk to people you admire, like, and respect. Ask if they are interested. Bring them together, have a conversation, and create it together. Be sure to set an intention for the group and create a process or structure so people don't feel their time is being wasted. I once participated in a pilot that was presented as a mastermind but in reality was a book club, that I would not have been interested in joining.

Have a clear purpose for the group and know why it exists. Invite the right people (you'll have to define your ideal mastermind participant as you did an ideal client), and set ground rules and expectations up front.

Search how to create a mastermind online. Tons of resources are available such as articles in Forbes and Lifehack as well as YouTube videos.

PILOTING GROUP COACHING

Kristin: An effective way to launch a group coaching program is to first offer a pilot. You can offer it at no charge or at an extremely discounted price to attract participants. Make sure these participants fit your target audience.

The benefits of a pilot are many, but the main value a pilot will bring are having testimonials upon launch, getting valuable feedback from participants to smooth out issues before charging full price for your program, and asking participants to place a dollar value on what they gained from the program. This last piece of feedback is helpful for pricing your offering.

For example, if you have six participants and they each suggest a dollar value they received from the program, you can average these amounts to produce a marketing pitch such as:

> *"Participants of [Title of Program] say they received an average value of $5,000 from the program. Yet you can join our transformational 12-week program for only $999. Following is what participants had to say about their experience…"*

As you can see, a pilot can yield valuable information to make your launch a bigger success since it has been tested.

PRICING GROUP COACHING

There isn't a set formula for pricing because there are too many variables, such as the coach's experience and skill level, geographic area, industry, size of an organization, and value of the work to the client. If you're solving a significant problem, people will be expecting and willing to pay more to solve the issue.

If you are pricing a project for an organization, they are used to higher price points. So, be careful not to under-charge because they will wonder if you have the skill level for the work. Pricing requires some experimentation.

My rates vary for group coaching. Here are some things to think about.

How many sessions and with how many people?

What is the size of the organization?

Will some one-on-one work be included?

Where is the group coaching taking place?

The larger the organization, the more I charge per person. You must remember that you have administrative costs that need to be covered and individuals in the group are significantly boosting their value learning new tools and approaches in the sessions. You are facilitating teaching that will pay dividends for as long as the person works for the organization.

If your group is for individuals who aren't in the same organization, your rate should be lower than an organizational rate, depending on the audience you're attracting. A workshop for unemployed jobseekers or students will be priced differently than for people in leadership roles.

If you include one-on-one time as part of the group program your price should take the individual time into account. One-one-one time is extremely valuable because the learning is targeted for that individual.

Will the coaching be in person, or virtual? In a specific geographic area, you may need to consider what people pay for these services in that area. For example, in large cities the cost will be higher. In smaller markets, people expect to pay less.

The more sessions and the more people, the more you charge. A group coaching series (six to eight sessions) for a large not-for-profit or a mid-size for profit might be charged between $4,500 and $6,000 per person. That is an all-inclusive rate – materials, assessments, facilitation, and one-on-one coaching sessions for each participant.

If you join a mastermind for coaches, there's a good chance others will share their pricing strategies so you can make better informed decisions.

My company charges close to the same rate for virtual group coaching as for in-person. It is just as much work. For in-person, you create handouts. For virtual, you create slides. We send these "packages" to the participants – sometimes before, sometimes after. If we want them to pay attention, we screen share and send the information after. If they need to write or do exercises, we send it in advance and ask them to print it out and bring it to the session.

Going virtual means you might need to learn new skills, such as how to skillfully navigate Zoom, Microsoft Teams or Google Meet, putting people in chat rooms, using all the functions, screen sharing, capturing notes, and doing a real-time survey. Honing these skills takes time, and time is money. You might choose to hire someone to do this for you, which adds to your costs.

Hopefully we've helped you figure out pricing

guidelines. When a coaching engagement ends, whether group or individual, how will you measure success? In the next chapter we'll address assessing success. Both yours and the client's.

22

——— ☓ ———

ASSESS SUCCESS:
YOURS & THE CLIENT'S
Kristin

Focusing solely on gaining and serving customers is a common mistake business owners make. Yes, clients are critical, but evaluating what's working, and not working, in your business is important to ensure customers return and also tell others about you. Repeat business and referrals are the lifeblood of a coaching business.

Evaluating success helps you and your future customers. Equipped with valuable information, you can make better decisions, implement change, expand on what's working well, and communicate objectively with prospective customers, creating increased interest in working with you.

In this chapter, I will share some of the ways you can measure success. A blend of qualitative and quantitative measures of success will give you and your clients a better picture of how you add value.

QUANTITATIVE SUCCESS

Quantitative means something that can be measured, counted, etc. You can count things like time and money, for example. Some of your successes can be quantified and some cannot. When something cannot be quantified or measured, we can assess quality instead, which is referred to as *qualitative*. Let's first take a look at two kinds of quantitative success measures.

Quantifiable Increases

Have your clients experienced an increase in college acceptance letters, job interviews, job offers, clients, monthly or annual revenue, salary, prospect-to-client conversions, promotions, mailing list or newsletter subscribers, social media followers, business investors or investment capital, employee retention or engagement scores, 360 evaluation scores, speaking engagements or speaking fees?

You have many options for tracking customer success, but you will need to ask questions to discover the client's starting point at the beginning of the engagement. Then, you'll also need to track their end point after the engagement has concluded. You can capture some of the starting point information in a coaching intake form, or you can ask questions as part of the discovery call or the first coaching session.

To track client success, you'll need to set up a process of monthly, quarterly, semi-annual, and/or annual check-ins.

Not all clients will contact you to share all their gains and wins, so you'll need to create a simple and repeatable outreach process. A spreadsheet for tracking can get you started, or you can use various apps or a database to track client data.

Your goal is to capture any metrics you need to measure before the work begins and then to set check-in periods after the engagement has ended. You can even track progress during the engagement, if that makes sense for you.

Once you've tracked some quantifiable increases, you can create meaningful marketing data to share in marketing materials, social media posts, website copy, and in discovery calls (see "Chapter 18: Discovery Calls" for more on managing discovery calls).

An example marketing statement based on client metric *increases* might look something like this:

Ninety-five percent of my clients receive a job offer within three weeks of working with me. The average job search takes 34 weeks, according to the Bureau of Labor Statistics.

Consider your best client experiences. What gains or *increases* can you quantifiably measure that you could begin to track and report?

Quantifiable Decreases

Depending on the solutions you provide to clients, decreases, not increases, might also be an indicator of success. Some desirable decreases are rejection letters, weeks spent unemployed, employee turnover, financial losses, overhead and expenses, average time to an offer, customer complaints, workplace injuries, regulatory violations, average time to market, and many more.

Example marketing statements based on client metric *decreases* might look something like this:

> My corporate clients report an average annual decrease in employee turnover of 17 percent after implementing an employee engagement and morale initiative.

> My job seeker clients report an average of six weeks unemployed, a decrease of 12 weeks from the average unemployed job seeker in the same industry.

Consider your best client experiences. What *decreases* can you quantifiably measure that you could begin to track and report?

QUALITATIVE SUCCESS

Qualitative Increases

Even qualitative success can be tracked. What are the qualitative outcomes you tend to provide to your clients. Think about your testimonials. What do clients say most about you? Do you increase their confidence? Do you get people unstuck and moving forward? Do they say you've given them hope?

If you track outcomes that don't have numbers or measurements you can still quantify your qualitative successes. Here is an example:

Ninety-eight percent of my clients report presenting with confidence in front of an audience after just one Communicate with Confidence coaching session.

What *qualitative increases* can you begin to track and report more quantifiably?

Qualitative Decreases

As with qualitative increases, you can track decreases the same way. What have you helped clients reduce, eliminate, or remove from their life? Do you help clients decrease anxiety, feelings of helplessness, grief, or loss? Do you reduce team conflict? Does your coaching decrease self-doubt or imposter syndrome?

Here is an example:

One hundred percent of couples I coach report they have fewer disagreements after completing my couples coaching program.

Fewer disagreements is not quantified, but number, average, or percentage of clients who report fewer disagreements is quantified. What *qualitative decreases* can you begin to track and report more quantitatively?

Data is compelling and powerful when shared with clients in discovery calls. You can share a client success statistic then back it up with a personal story related to the prospective client's desired outcome. Repurpose this same data and story for a newsletter or social media post. If you are a new coach and lack experience, one idea is to offer discounted or pro bono coaching to a handful of people in your network. You can exchange coaching for an honest testimonial and the completion of a short survey about the experience of working with you.

I once met a marriage counselor at a networking event who told our group she had a 93 percent success rate with her intensive counseling program for couples dealing with infidelity. I can't remember the success rate of traditional marriage counseling but I recall her success was significantly higher.

Now it's time to capture ways you can begin measuring client success.

ACTIVITY:

Brainstorm as many quantitative and qualitative successes you can think of for your clients that you can begin tracking. Review your client testimonials for ideas.

Statistics are powerful motivators for prospective clients who want comparable results. Just because your client experiences success doesn't mean you will feel successful. Client satisfaction surely matters. Still, you must define what success looks like for *you*. Consider your values. How do they influence the way you will measure your own success? What does that look like? Quality of connection with clients? Status as an expert? Stress level? Enough time for exercise and recreation with family? What does success look like for *you?*

You might recall Laura's story told earlier in the book. I shared how she coaches executives at a Fortune 100 ranked company. Despite success on paper, Laura did not feel fulfilled. Success comes down to fulfillment.

Refer to your values on your *Coach Canvas* from *The Four Pillars of Career Fit*™ exercises. Your values have the greatest influence on how you view your success.

ACTIVITY:

Consider your criteria for both quantitative and qualitative success as a coach. What does success look like for you? Do you need to make any changes to feel more successful?

_____

_____

_____

_____

_____

_____

_____

_____

As you consider success, have you identified any struggles running your business? Are you unable to serve larger clients as a solopreneur? Partnerships might interest you.

23

CঞB

PARTNERSHIPS

Judi

Contracting, partnering, and collaborating with other coaches is worth exploring but won't be right for everyone. An example of a win/win collaboration is when you, or another coach, have a client project that is too extensive to execute with the resources you have, such as time and people.

As an example, let's say you have a client who manages a department of twenty-five people. This client wants you, the coach, to provide assessments to his or her team and meet individually with each person to debrief assessment results. After the debriefs are completed, the client wants you to lead a workshop with the team.

Depending on your schedule, some team members might have an undesirable wait time to get on your calendar for a debrief. If the workshop date has been set, this could cause you to scramble to get all the debriefs completed prior to the group workshop. This example illustrates when bringing a contract coach onto your project could be helpful.

Collaborating with others usually brings pros and cons. Consider if you need a partner for the short-term, such as one project, or on a regular basis, which could make the need long-term. Following are important questions to think about. We'll share our thoughts for you to consider as you plan and make decisions.

How do I decide if partnering is something I want to do?

Here are six ways partnering can benefit you:

1. *Exit strategy* – Is partnering an element of your exit strategy? Do you want to partner with a person or persons who might be interested in buying your practice at some point?

2. *Volume* – Do you have more work than you can currently handle, or do you have some big projects coming up where it would be helpful to have another person?

3. *Back-up* – What if you are sick, have an emergency, or want to go on vacation? Do you have someone who can step in and handle things for you?

4. *Expenses* – If you partner with someone, you can keep more of your profit because you have someone who can help pay expenses – rent, bookkeeping, supplies and so forth.

5. *Intellectual Property* – Do you plan to (or would you like to) co-develop intellectual property or new services or even ways to creatively conduct your work? The old saying "two heads are better than one" is true when it comes to

brainstorming or problem-solving. Your partner may also have experience or skills you lack and can help round out business offerings.

6. *Collaboration* – Coaches are often relationship-oriented and some may have the *helper* career code. They truly prefer working with people versus working alone and value having another person they can talk to who understands what the business is going through. Being a business owner of any kind can be lonely. This person can also serve as an "informal" coach for *you*. You might also struggle to have an independent practice and need a partner who has strengths you don't have like budgeting, Statements of Work (SOWs), and tax preparation.

How do I choose who to partner with?

Primarily, it should be someone you know. If you invite a person to work with you on the occasional project, you can "road test" what it could be like if you worked together. Equally important is sharing values. Your values should be aligned. Why does she coach? Is her reason similar to yours? Does she have the same sense of ethics? What is her long-term game plan? Finally, refer to our trust framework in "Chapter 19: Coaching Process & Best Practices." Do you trust this person?

You are going to be sharing something really important with her, and you will spend a fair amount of time together. You will work better together if your skills and personality traits complement each other. Don't rush. Take your time. I'm a huge fan of piloting things to see if they work.

On top of all this, create a legal agreement. You may be grateful at some point to have a document that clearly spells out the relationship and who is entitled to what. Review this document with the lawyer(s) who drafted it so everyone is clear from the beginning what's involved. There are no details too small. Get good legal advice.

How can I head off potential problems?

Communicate. Talk about things before they become a problem. If you don't feel comfortable doing this, or you shy away from it, there is not enough trust. Road test giving one another feedback before you form a partnership of any kind, especially a legal one. If you can't do this, don't go into business with him.

How do I maintain the relationship(s)

Again, communicate. Set aside time each week for a check-in conversation. A wonderful way to do this is over breakfast or lunch. Talk early and often. Share your deepest hopes, dreams, and concerns with each other. Make sure you have a strong bond. Stay in touch. Don't let the demands of the business rob you of this critical ritual. If you do, you will grow apart and that's the beginning of trouble.

What if things go wrong? How do I get back on track?

Not to sound like a broken record – communicate. Use your weekly check-in meeting to explore what you are thinking and feeling. Do it early when the problem is still small. Be prepared to have a conversation that might feel uncomfortable at first. It will get easier as you organize your thoughts. Demonstrate willingness to listen and genuine caring for your colleague.

We've given you an extensive list of questions in "Chapter 20: Assessments & Tools." Look through these questions. Which ones do you want to bring to this important conversation? For starters, you might choose the two basics – what's working in our arrangement? What might we do better, differently, more of? If you and your chosen colleague have similar values, ethics and approaches to the work, you may discover your concern/issue/potential problem is shared!

Have an exit strategy

Steven Covey famously said, "Begin with the end in mind" and that's the point of an exit strategy. Know before you even start how you want to end. You don't necessarily need a date, but some type of time frame is helpful. You can always extend it. Be sure to include at least the framework for this in your agreement to work together and discuss it with your potential colleague(s). A great rule of thumb is "no surprises." You could consider an annual review – how are things going? Ask your potential colleague(s) for their thoughts about how to work out this important detail.

Coaching and consulting partnerships are an effective method to expand your business and attract larger coaching and consulting opportunities. Support is essential for large contracts. Hopefully, the above questions have helped you decide if this is right for you.

As we pointed out, successful partnerships can expand your influence and business opportunities. You might think you need a partnership because you are too busy to run a business by yourself. Before you make that decision, ensure you are managing your time effectively. Time management is a struggle for many people.

24

― ෆ ―

TIME MANAGEMENT

Kristin

As you establish or grow a business, you should structure your business to work best for you and your life. It would be presumptuous to dictate how to run your business; however, aligning your business and your time to your values is necessary if you intend to be happy and fulfilled as a business owner. Refer to your *Coach Canvas* to review your values. If you haven't yet completed the "My Top Values" exercise, you can find it in "Chapter 2: You, the Coach."

Your business will grow a mind of its own and start running *you* if you don't set your intentions and shape your business how you want it. For example, if you value balance, health, or connection with loved ones, arrange your business to *integrate* with other important priorities such as your exercise routine, picking up the kids from school, travel, or hobbies.

In this chapter I cover seven areas to help you manage your time and build a business that brings you more joy than pain. These areas are work/life integration, time bandits, schedule management, client load, prioritization, the "Genius Spiral," and smart networking.

WORK/LIFE INTEGRATION

If working long hours isn't appealing, establish habits for work/life integration. Following are ideas to get you started. Add your ideas, as well. Choose one or two to try now, then add another once habits are established.

- Start your morning with exercise to manage stress
- Try meditation or yoga for renewed daily focus
- Create a plan to encourage focused effort
- Block your calendar to prevent meeting overload
- Invest time to create passive income, such as products
- Create templates and processes to save time
- Create DIY resources to help others "at a distance"
- Write blogs or a book to share knowledge at scale
- Learn new skills that add value or reduce frustration
- Outsource tasks that cause burn out
- Try a virtual assistant a few hours each week
- Build relationships strategically with target clients
- Put your phone in a different room for better sleep
- Set limits on screen time
- Schedule social media breaks to foster productivity
- Reduce or eliminate time wasters during the day

My first two to three years in business, I chose to work long hours each week (80 hours on average and as many as 100) to increase the likelihood of success. Three years later, I started to build passive income. The upfront time investment now enables me to work fewer than 40 hours each week, take summers off, and has doubled my company's revenue this year over last.

The amount of time you invest in your business is a personal decision. If you have a family, you'll need to discuss what is going to work best for your situation. Whether you choose to prioritize your time across multiple areas of life or choose to be laser focused on your business, always keep in mind that hugely successful people are *intentional*.

TIME BANDITS

Coaches, consultants, and business owners must be aware of time wasters, known as time bandits. Examples are failure to delegate, interruptions, procrastination, email, low priority tasks, constant cell phone checking, clutter and disorganization, not setting daily goals, perfectionism, and repetitive tasks.

Following are time mastery tips I've found helpful. I will elaborate on items that warrant deeper discussion. I have also created a playlist containing brief videos with actionable time management tips, here: bit.ly/rscvideos.

TIME MASTERY TIPS

Track your time – Write down how you spend your time for one week to identify if you engage in too many low priority tasks and time wasters. This reveals where you need to make adjustments. Activity tracking is a wonderful starting point because you can identify areas for improvement rather than making changes that are less impactful.

Set goals each day – Write down, the previous evening, what you want to accomplish each day. Stating our intentions of what we must complete each day improves productivity. I have learned that if I don't set goals, busy work and demands of the day start calling the shots. The tail wags the dog, so to speak.

Prioritize – Don't simply write a to-do list, decide your three to five top priorities on your list each day. Add high priority tasks to the top of the to-do list. If you don't complete some of the items, move them to the top of the following day's list.

A to-do list helps you stay focused and accomplish more. A *prioritized* to-do list helps you achieve greater *impact*. We provide an "Impact/Effort" prioritization tool, and explain how to use it, later in this chapter.

Learn to Say "No" – Set criteria for when you will say no. For example, ask yourself two questions: "Do I have time to do this?" and "Am I the best person to do this?" If the answer to either question is no, the answer is no. You can even ask; "Do I want to do this?"

Check in with your *Coach Canvas* you created in "Part I: Ready," when needed. Does the request fit your strengths, preferred skills, values and personality-based interests? Is the requester your ideal client? Does the request align with your motivation? Is it aligned to your experience? Maybe you just don't want to get involved. That's a sufficient reason to say no. Let your "no" be no. A song and dance explanation isn't required. "I appreciate you thinking of me. I will need to decline this time."

Limit distractions – Create friction or barriers to limit your distractions, such as placing your phone in airplane mode or leaving your device in another room while you tackle your to-do list. Turn notifications off on your phone during time dedicated to carrying out a task. I have all social media notifications permanently turned off.

Get organized to simplify your life – Disorganization is a major cause of wasted time. Declutter and simplify your workspace and keep your computer files organized. More guidance on this topic can be found in the video playlist.

Delegate – Anything that's not an effective use of your time should be delegated whenever possible. The decluttering video and "The Genius Spiral" covered later in this chapter will help.

Maximize productivity – When are you most productive during the day? Timing matters. Pay attention to when you are most and least productive and plan important tasks accordingly. More guidance on this topic can be found in the video playlist.

Set boundaries – To minimize interruptions, set boundaries with yourself and others. When working from home, if your office door is closed, you are at work and should only be interrupted for emergencies. Define what an emergency is! Boundaries can also include only going on your cell phone during designated breaks.

Find the root of procrastination – Procrastination isn't laziness, it's avoidance. Make a list of the things you tend to avoid. Why do you avoid them? Can you delegate, stop doing, change how you do the task to make it more enjoyable, or hire someone else? What does your *Coach Canvas* reveal about why you are procrastinating?

Manage email – When we constantly check email, we are reactive. It generally takes up to 20 minutes to regain focus after an interruption. Set breaks during your day for checking email, and turn off notifications to get out of "react mode."

Eliminate/reduce repetitive tasks – What tasks do you find yourself doing over and over? Turn the tasks into templates. Do you send similar emails repeatedly like proposals, coaching session follow-ups, accountability emails, etc.?

Something created once that can be quickly changed for other situations will save not only *your* time but an admin's time as well.

Done is better than perfect – Perfectionism is self-defeating. Is obsessive tinkering of your website or LinkedIn profile adding real value to your business?

"Research shows that perfectionism hampers success. In fact, it's often the path to depression, anxiety, addiction, and life paralysis." – Brené Brown

---

How many of the 13 tips do you currently practice regularly? How would you rate yourself on each tip from 1 to 10? One is you are being crushed and 10 you are crushing it.

Again, this playlist contains videos with actionable tips to help: bit.ly/rscvideos.

SCHEDULE MANAGEMENT

Another strategy to manage your time more effectively is schedule blocking. Early in my coaching business I began using a time scheduling app, and I set it up to allow appointments between 9:45 a.m. and 3:00 p.m., and again from 6:00 p.m. until 9:00 p.m. for clients in different time zones or who worked during the day. No other restrictions were put in place.

On multiple occasions, I'd check my schedule for the coming day and find six to eight meetings on my calendar. I also had client deliverables, writing, and other deadlines and began to feel like a prisoner to phone calls. Not only was there no time for my own priorities, but no energy remained to work on those tasks after so many hours of meetings.

Before long, I realized being reactive to my schedule was not sustainable. I began blocking off every Monday and Friday. This allowed me to take off long weekends without rescheduling anything. It also gave me time on the first day of the week to wrap up deliverables for clients that were due that week. At the end of the week, I could complete outstanding tasks to eliminate or reduce the need to work on weekends.

Look ahead to the coming months and proactively block time for yourself first. Whether you block time for writing, content creation, planning, goal achievement, daily exercise, or meet ups with colleagues and friends, schedule time to create cushion and space to avoid stress and burnout.

CLIENT LOAD

A consistent theme in this book is *intention*. If you don't set intentions in all areas of your business, as I said before, the tail begins to wag the dog. I remember a time when I was carrying 24 individual coaching clients at the same time, and it was exhausting. Most days felt intense and stressful. The next day I'd wake up and do it all over again.

In the early days of any coaching practice, gaining clients is often the primary goal. In time, as your practice grows, you can define your sweet spot for the number of customers you can joyfully serve with high quality.

Notice how you're feeling from week to week. You might not know how many clients you can manage at the same time, but your body is keeping score. Set a practice of doing a weekly check in with yourself.

How did my client load feel this week?
Was I overextended, making it difficult to meet deadlines?
Was the volume of my meetings this week comfortable?

When finding your optimal client load, ensure your time estimate to serve a client takes at least these three things into account:

1. *Prep time* – Includes reviewing resources, documentation, dedicated time for learning, research, proposal preparation, communications, administration, and any other up front time investment needed to serve a client.

2. *Coaching time* – Includes time spent with a client.

3. *Follow up* – Includes post-session communications, client follow-up, administration, deliverables and action items.

Consider how much time you plan to devote to clients, including both direct and indirect time. If you're spending all day with clients, other activities like research, follow-up, deliverables, learning, and administration will cause your work to creep into each evening and weekend.

Time should be distributed to not only working *in* your business (serving customers) but working *on* your business. As you consider how much time to give to customers each week, consider other priorities that might compete for your time, such as:

- Business strategy and planning
- Building and deepening your skills
- Managing and solving problems
- Creating intellectual property
- Content creation
- Social media
- Marketing efforts
- Networking
- Tax preparation
- Website content

How to Prioritize

How do you know what to prioritize in your business? Try implementing an impact/effort grid.

Impact: Will it help to achieve your goals?
Effort: What resources are needed to get the job done?

Following is a process to create an Impact/Effort Grid to help you prioritize tackling your tasks and activities. Start by defining the criteria for evaluating your business activities.

1. *Define Your Goal*: This could be a business goal, a project goal, a personal life goal, etc.

   e.g. *Increase revenue by 50 percent*

2. *Define Impact*: How much impact does the task or activity contribute to achieving the stated goal? For example:

   High Impact – Surpasses your goal. e.g. *60 percent revenue increase*

   Medium Impact – Achieves your goal. e.g. *50 percent revenue increase*

   Low Impact – Does not achieve your goal. e.g. *<50 percent revenue increase*

3. *Define Effort:* How much will it cost in terms of time, money, people or other resources? For example:

   High Effort: It could take several weeks or months, it's not in your budget, and you need people beyond you to help. e.g. *longer than 3 months; no $ available*

   Medium Effort: It could take a few weeks, it's within your budget but a lot of money, and you need others to help you. e.g. *two weeks; $750 of budget*

   Low Effort: It could take a few hours or days, it won't cost much, and it's completely within your control. e.g. *two hours; no $ cost*

Next, list activities associated with your work or life. Go through your list, decide the impact and effort of each and enter them into the Impact/Effort Grid.

Increase Revenue by 50 Percent

		Low	Medium	High
IMPACT	*High*	1		2
	Medium		3	
	Low	4		5
		Low	*Medium*	*High*
			EFFORT	

Once you have each task distributed to a section, it's time to analyze your results. Each number in the grid above represents a task and is explained in the following table. Prioritize your next steps based on the description under *Action Steps*.

SECTION	ACTION STEPS
1: High Impact/Low Effort	*Quick Hits!* Start here. These are easy tasks to help surpass your goal.
2: High Impact/High Effort	*Plan for the Future* These are major tasks that take a lot of effort with big payoff. These might require more planning or people.
3: Medium Impact/ Medium Effort	*Options, Options, Options* These activities offer promise, but require work. Spread these out over time or delegate them.
4: Low Impact/Low Effort	*Low Hanging Fruit* You might feel Low Impact activities should be ignored. Sometimes they're needed for a quick win. Consider them carefully but stay focused on High Impact activities.
5: Low Impact/High Effort	*Why Bother?* Think twice before doing tasks that rob resources with low payoff. Perhaps someone important asked you to undertake these tasks. Show her the high payoff/low effort tasks you've identified.
Other Squares	*Use Your Judgment* Decide for each task. In general, High Impact tasks are the best place to begin.

Managing time effectively hinges on knowing how to prioritize. Is there anything you need to start doing differently?

THE GENIUS SPIRAL

Many of us spend too much time on activities that do not leverage our talents or give us the best return on our time investment. A variety of reasons explain why, including failure to delegate and not being aware of one's talents. Author and psychologist, Gay Hendricks, created an enlightening concept called *The Genius Spiral*.

Zone of GENIUS!	Zone of Excellence
Zone of Competence	Zone of Incompetence

Zone of Incompetence – things most others do better than we can. We should never operate in the Zone of Incompetence.

Zone of Competence – things we do as well as many others. We should limit or eliminate time spent in this zone.

Zone of Excellence – things we do better than most others. We persist in them long after we've achieved proficiency, and the work becomes routine. Many people stay here.

Zone of Genius – the place of flow. We are energized and

excited by what we're doing. We are fully absorbed, using the full range of our gifts.

We live more powerful, fulfilled, and happy lives when we spend as much time as possible in our Zone of Genius. Remember these zones as you plan your time and set goals.

Idea for Action *Discover Your Zone of Genius*

Give yourself permission to discover your areas of genius. Make a commitment to spend time in this zone by finding one thing you enjoy most. Be open to failure and schedule 15 minutes daily devoted to this area of genius. Check out *The Big Leap* and *The Joy of Genius* by Gay Hendricks to go deeper on this topic, and remember to refer back to *The Four Pillars of Career Fit*™ in "Chapter 2: You, the Coach."

SMARTER NETWORKING

Networking can be an effective business development tool, but it is a double-edged sword since it is also a chief time bandit. If you have a presence on social media, putting yourself in the public eye will invite more requests for networking calls. If you are an extrovert, it could be tempting to accept every invitation to network that you receive, especially if you want to grow your business.

Be mindful of your time and remember the majority of people who ask to meet with you aren't looking to grow or advance *your* business, they're often seeking to advance their own interests.

Following are three ways to avoid unnecessary meetings:

#1: Budget your networking time

Set aside time each week for networking meetings, such as three hours. You have flexibility in how you spend this time. In some instances, you could dedicate 30 minutes to a person you're willing to meet with but who is not in your target audience.

In other cases you might devote a full hour to someone if a mutually beneficial relationship seems obvious. Once you use up your allotted networking time for the week, begin scheduling people for the following week. When the next week fills, schedule meetings two weeks out, and so on. Be prepared to respond, "My next available networking appointment is one month from now." You can also reserve one 30-minute spot each week for "urgent" and highly desirable networking meetings.

Regardless of how your networking allocation is set up, honor the budget you created. Otherwise, your process is merely show and won't accomplish what you created it to do: *respect your time.*

#2: Create criteria for when to accept or decline requests

In "Chapter 4: Your Ideal Clients," we guided you through steps to clarify who you want to work with. You can approach networking similarly to define high-quality networking partners. I have included an activity in this chapter to create your criteria for high-value networking partners.

For example, I help coaches, consultants and leaders, and also write children's books aimed at building confidence through self-awareness. Therefore, my high-value networking partners include people working in Human Resources, consultants and coaches, educators in elementary education through college and university, and those working directly with children or who serve in an organization geared toward helping children.

What are the characteristics of
your high-quality networking partner?

#3: Decline 99 percent of requests

My preference is to first establish communication and build rapport prior to having a networking call, unless I have been introduced to someone for a specific purpose. If someone I don't know sends a message requesting a "get-to-know-each-other" meeting in the first outreach I decline unless the message and the individual's profile suggests he or she is a high-quality networking partner.

Otherwise, I reply indicating I keep communications on the social media platform and move to live communication if it makes sense for us after we have interacted. When I receive cold sales pitches requesting my time, I archive the message and sometimes disconnect. Removing a connection might seem harsh, but sales people will target my connections to influence others to accept his or her request.

 ACTIVITY:

Reflect on who you serve.

Consider organizations, potential partners, even coaches or consultants who serve your clients in a different capacity by meeting a different need.

List the kinds of people you would like to network with in the space supplied to develop a criteria for accepting networking requests.

Consider proactively reaching out to people in your network that align with your criteria for high-quality networking partners.

 Explain *why* you are reaching out to request time. Connect the dots why it makes sense to speak.

Did you hear her on a podcast?

Did you view her profile and find common interests?

Did she write a book on a topic of mutual interest?

Periodically review your high-value networking partner criteria. Revise as your business evolves or your needs change.

Hopefully, you feel equipped to manage the networking time bandit. I devoted a lot of time to the subject because it's a common issue that coaches don't often address until hours of time have already been lost.

I packed a lot into this chapter to help you take control of your time. Use what works and hold off on anything that feels overwhelming.

The next chapter, "Passive Income & Intellectual Property," is a game changer. Creating passive income sets you on a path to financial and schedule freedom and enables you to increase generosity. Intellectual property establishes expertise and paves the way to higher rates and revenue.

25

❦

PASSIVE INCOME & INTELLECTUAL PROPERTY
Kristin

Passive income refers to revenue generated without your time and presence needed. Passive income is an effective way to supplement your earnings and supply flexibility in the number of clients you accept, hours you work, number of days off you can afford to take, and more.

Intellectual property elevates your reputation by positioning you as an expert or authority in your field. Intellectual property can also be used to generate passive income, in addition to moving you to the forefront within your network. The combination of developing passive income and intellectual property expands your influence and revenue. The more influence and revenue you create, the more freedom and autonomy you gain.

Even if you aren't motivated by influence or money, freedom appeals to most of us. The door also swings open wider to help more people as you solidify your position as an authority in your field.

PASSIVE INCOME

Burn out is a common occurrence in the coaching and consulting industry. While being busy can be a great problem to have with clients and referrals continually knocking at your door, eighty-hour work weeks can quickly become a reality.

Working long hours week after week is not always sustainable. As the saying goes, "Don't tie your time to your dime." Tying your time to your dime simply means you must be directly present or involved in every dollar you earn. Passive income creates space, more room to breathe.

Earning money while you sleep sounds pretty great, right? In 2018, I decided to focus the majority of my efforts on building a variety of passive income channels to reduce working hours and spend more time with family.

Passive income affords me an ability to travel on a more flexible schedule, engage in month-long writing sabbaticals, and work limited hours over the summer to travel and visit out-of-town family.

When starting my business, I only offered career coaching services. Coaching is a competitive space, so early on I thought about how to differentiate myself from other coaches. I decided the best solution for me was innovation given I have four *thinking* strengths. My approach would be the creation of products, tools and content since these things also align to my skills and interests. We talked about our personality-based *interests* expressing through our *skills* back in "Chapter 2: You, the Coach." This is a wonderful time to revisit your interests and preferred skills to design a passive income approach that will work best for you. I decided to create a product store on my website.

My plan was to break down the work I was doing with clients and create a framework other coaches and consultants could eventually use to help their clients. A need existed in the market because many coaches weren't using a clear framework or method and were patching together a process. This framework is now known as YouMap®, the assessment and the accompanying coaching framework mentioned in "Chapter 20: Assessments & Tools."

What need do you see in the market that you might fill?

Next, I wrote books laying out my methods step-by-step to create avenues of self-help. For example, both coaches and job seekers tend to read my career book, *YouMap*. I also wrote a book called *Your Team Loves Mondays...Right?* to support managers in building their management skills. When I was in management, and also coaching a high potential leadership pipeline, I created a number of tools such as an employee development framework. I included this and other tools in the book. Self-help programs and products are excellent passive income generators.

The next step was to create training programs to teach other people to use these frameworks. To support expansion of the training programs, I created a Master Trainer process to teach other coaches to certify people in YouMap®. This was a huge step as now people can be certified by other Master Trainers, not just me, which expands the reach of the certification.

After these elements were in place, I created new, yet related, products to spread into new demographics. The first addition was a do-it-yourself (DIY) YouMap® profile anyone could buy from our online store. We saw an increase in recruiters ordering profiles to send to employers to show candidate fit. Job seekers who didn't have the budget for coaching could now bring their YouMap® to an interview to stand out from the other candidates and increase the chance of an offer.

Growth continued into more demographics. I collaborated with my designer to build the YouMap® Youth and YouMap® Teen profiles to reach people earlier in life, building confidence through self-awareness. I went a step further and developed parent and teacher companion guides to help adults gain more value from these resources. Caregivers now have actionable ideas and guidance to reinforce a child's strengths, values, preferred skills, and interests in their day-to-day lives.

As a future step, I could expand into courses for the LinkedIn learning platform or other eLearning platforms. I could create training programs and webinars for student and corporate YouMap® workshops. I can continue to create video content and monetize my YouTube channel.

Newsletters are also a solid vehicle to share high value content with subscribers if writing or speaking on video are within your preferred skills. James Clear's first book, *Atomic Habits*, became a massive best seller largely because he had already built a following from his newsletter over a two-year period.

Content you create could be set up on a subscription platform such as Patreon. Consistency is key to building a following. Most people end up quitting an initiative, such as a YouTube channel, too early when they become discouraged by the data in the first few weeks or months. Creators who push through are the ones who experience success.

Passive income opportunities are almost endless. If you create at minimum a half dozen passive income channels, you experience a snowball effect. One source might not produce significant revenue, but six channels combined can generate a tidy sum. *Think about achieving economies of scale. Create passive income ideas that build off each other and are thematically related.*

For example, when you create content and intellectual property, writing a book is easier because you aren't recreating the wheel or building on completely unrelated topics.

The approach I have outlined to creating passive income is transferable to other roles and industries. I hope what I shared sparks ideas. Allow your mind to wander and avoid shooting down your ideas as they birth. Write them down. Give them space to grow.

INTELLECTUAL PROPERTY

As said previously, creating intellectual property can level up your position as an expert in the eyes of others. A sound reason to create intellectual property is your client's perception and experience. Intellectual property positions you as a leader and a creator in your customer's mind. But that doesn't mean you should recreate the wheel.

Leverage existing content where it makes sense, expand or repurpose other content, always giving proper attribution. The *Coach Canvas* I created and made available for you in the *Appendix* was changed and expanded upon with attribution for the original work included. Build new tools, processes, workbooks, exercises or activities to supplement your coach toolkit. Having your own intellectual property positions you as a thought leader.

There's also another practical reason to create intellectual property. I started writing books because I was asked the same questions over and over. The sole reason I wrote *5 Surprising Steps to Land the Job NOW!* was because of the many messages on LinkedIn asking a variation of, "I have a job interview tomorrow. Do you have any tips or advice?"

I responded saying, "That question doesn't have a quick answer!" People were looking for quick tips, so I decided to write the book as a short and easy read that one could skim for high-impact tips before an interview.

What questions are you continually asked?
Create a shareable resource to answer questions at scale.

Rather than typing out the same responses or repeatedly hearing yourself share the same guidance on calls and video chats, create a reusable resource you can share with a link. One of my favorite websites is bitly.com which allows you to create a repository of custom URLs for all your resources to readily share them. Not only that, but you can reference Bitly links *within* your resources to make it easier for clients to access linked sites or files within those resources. Bitly also provides data including how often your links are clicked.

I have many of my most commonly shared Bitly links memorized. Bitly links are also great for including links when they aren't clickable, such as within Instagram posts and stories, or your LinkedIn about section. The URLs should be made as short and memorable as possible so it's simple for people to type into a browser. The URLs are case-sensitive so you should mention this to people as you share them.

As an example, I created custom Bitly links for my children's book series. As I mentioned, if you memorize your most in-demand resources it saves time digging up URLs when you want to send them to someone. I recommend using a naming convention so related resources are similar. Following is an example:

You've Got Gifts! – bit.ly/youvegotgifts
You've Got Values! – bit.ly/youvegotvalues
You've Got Skills! – bit.ly/youvegotskills
You've Got Personality! – bit.ly/youvegotpersonality
You've Got Quirks! – bit.ly/youvegotquirks

If you're not interested in writing a book, you could create webinars, videos, courses, blogs, articles, short eBooks, or anything you can reuse and share. Resources can be used for paid clients, marketing content, or simply to help others.

Consider creating intellectual property or developing a formal process for what you do well. Maybe you have already created intellectual property and it simply needs some branding.

Gina Riley is a career transition coach who helps legacy-minded leaders and executives customize their career story to land high impact jobs. She has created a comprehensive, step-by-step framework called *Career Velocity*. Her nine-step system is a roadmap for leaders, executives, and CXOs.

Gina says that creating *Career Velocity* helped her fine tune her service offering and who she uniquely serves to attract the right clients. We've reinforced the importance of attracting the right clients repeatedly by this point.

Gina explained that going through this process gave her confidence to explain, sell, and persuade target clients that she has a framework that works. Gina now converts more strategy calls into paying clients and has achieved a six-figure revenue by having a method.

Is it time to get your process or idea into the world?

ACTIVITY:

Do you have a process? How many steps does it have?

Write the core steps of your process.

Brainstorm a name for your framework, method, or system.

_____

_____

_____

_____

_____

_____

_____

You can begin using a trademark symbol (™) at once (in the United States) with no fees or applications needed. Apply for a registered mark (®) through the U.S. Patent Office. Once your mark is approved, you can swap the ™ for the ® on all your materials and marketing efforts.

Before applying for a registered mark, search the Trademark Electronic Search System (TESS) to check if someone has already registered a name in the same domain. The trademark search link is below and also in the *Appendix*. The same name can be registered and approved as long as they are in different domains.

For example, YouMap® is registered to me in two different classes in the coaching and counseling space. YouMap® is also registered in two different non-competing classes as an application software that supplies geographic information based on user interests. This is someone else's trademark.

U.S. Patent Office Trademark Search:
http://tess2.uspto.gov

Once you have your system in place, the intellectual property you have created is fertile ground for creating all sorts of passive income streams.

 Create a course, video, book, or product to sell based on your system. Allow yourself to dream a bit! Make a list of values-aligned goals and consider what you could do with more freedom. Let those ideas motivate you to create passive income. What first step will you take?

Many coaches are interested in earning extra income through speaking. If that interests you, continue to the next chapter.

26

⁓ ℭℬ ⁓

SPEAKING ENGAGEMENTS

Kristin

Are you interested in getting your message to the masses? Speaking can be an effective way to show your expertise, attract your tribe, humanize your work, give back to your community, increase your visibility, inform, inspire, and attract clients.

Coaches have told me they want to speak but don't consider themselves an expert in anything. In "Chapter 2: You, the Coach," one of the exercises in "The 3 C's of Coaching" section was listing your background and experiences. *Your lived experiences are your expertise. Apply topics of interest to your stories then share practical lessons with the audience.*

Earlier in my career, I said yes to almost everyone who asked me to speak and, in hindsight, that was a mistake. Everything you say yes to requires you to say no to other things. Time is finite, so there is always an opportunity cost when we choose one way to spend our time over another.

Remember in "Chapter 4: Your Ideal Clients," I walked you through how to figure out your ideal clients? Later, in

"Chapter 24: Time Management," I also had you think about high value partners. Before saying yes to a speaking engagement, you'll want to ask a few questions.

If your ideal clients and/or high value partners will be in attendance at an event, it will be worth your while to speak, even pro bono. If your high value partners and ideal clients are not present, you'll want to decline the request.

To figure out if your ideal clients or high value partners will be in attendance, you can ask questions about the purpose of the event. Who are the attendees? What are their backgrounds and professions?

Second, are participants being charged a fee to attend the event? More often these days I get asked to speak for free at events where the organizer is charging an event fee, which means they are generating revenue on my expertise, as well as others. A hard no will be given for that request.

If the event is organized by a non-profit with a cause I care about, I am more likely to say yes if there is a nominal fee to cover costs, such as renting the venue. I am unlikely to speak for a profit-based organization that is charging participants unless it is a paid speaking engagement.

SPEAKING FEES

Coaches often want to know what to charge for speaking fees. As with pro bono requests for your services, you should ask, "Does your event have a budget for speaking fees?" It will then be clear up front if you're being asked to offer pro bono speaking.

Harvard Business Review offers the following pricing guidance on speaking fees. New or inexperienced speakers might earn $500–$2,500 for a talk. If your talk is for a group of recent graduates, you can expect an honorarium or speaker fee toward the $500 end of the continuum. If you are speaking to a group of senior executives, you would lean toward the $2,500 end of the pay scale. Who you are speaking to influences the speaker fee.

Speakers establishing a brand based on a first book could earn $5,000–$10,000 for a speaking event with a decent-sized crowd.

An author with several books and other forms of social proof, such as a large following on social media, might draw $10,000–$20,000.

Those who are very well-known in their field, such as best-selling authors, can bring in $20,000–$35,000 per talk.

You'll notice books are often mentioned. You are more likely to command speaker fees if you are a published author or if you're an entrepreneur who has created a product or program with some familiarity in the marketplace.

I remember attending an annual Women in Business professional development event early in my entrepreneurial career, before I published any books. I approached the president of the organization that put on the event and expressed interest in speaking at a future event. My offer fell flat.

A couple years later, I published my first book, which was based on the research of Valerie Murray and the *Five Success Factors for Women*. Valerie granted permission to write about her research, allowing me to explain the model, her research, and offer development advice to nurture the five factors.

When the book was about to release, I contacted the same organization behind the annual Women in Business event and explained my new book was coming out. I also offered free digital copies to Women in Business members. Within 20 minutes, the president called me from her car on route to a meeting and extended an invitation for a keynote.

I suppose since writing a book is a lot of work and requires discipline and follow-through, I became more attractive as a speaker. I was invited back to speak at least three or four times after that event.

After delivering one particular keynote, they allowed me to sell my books on a table at the back of the room. I brought copies of four different books which promptly sold out. When people are feeling inspired by your talk, they want more from you and will often buy a book. If you're interested in writing a book, we cover this topic in the next chapter.

In addition to selling out the books, I received an email after the event. One of the participants referred me for a paid speaking event at a university close to where I live. The talk was part of a larger professional development initiative for the entire staff and faculty with the provost and president in attendance.

After concluding that talk, I was approached for a consulting opportunity at Newell Brands which owns Rubbermaid®, Graco®, Oster®, and over 40 other well-known brands. I was brought in to do strengths workshops with Rubbermaid® and, later, Quickie®. Speaking engagements can create ripple effects of paid work.

SPEAKING TIPS

Great public speakers have a few things in common. They know their audience, have a clear purpose in the message, present with authenticity instead of trying to be someone else, and influence through narration.

When speaking, rather than put your audience to sleep with slides and statistics, make your point through a story. You lived the experience, you know it, and you felt it. Now help others feel it and move them with it. At the end of your talk, distill your experience into one to three practical lessons, tips, or actions the audience can apply to their lives. Whenever I speak, event organizers tell me the same thing: *Audience members want actionable tips they can apply.* This is not surprising since application is one of the eight principles of adult learning.[14]

Following are some other speaking tips:

- Speak on topics you know well
- Tell engaging stories
- Words should be plain, short, and specific
- Use pauses to add power
- Avoid a monotonous tone by varying pitch; speak with emphasis, inflection, and enthusiasm
- Add variety through change of pace (tempo)
- Silence the distracted voice in your head
- Speak with ease, forwardness, and openness
- Be yourself; let your personality come through
- Use moderate gestures, not too many
- Stand poised but flexible
- Join a public speaking club to practice

In addition to speaking, another way to expand your influence and revenue is through writing books. I will cover this topic in the next chapter.

27

C3

BOOK WRITING

Kristin

Writing a book is a long and often challenging process. It's a lot of work – arduous work. I had to gut and re-write an entire third of this book while going through the developmental edit. That doesn't sound very encouraging, does it? If you've ever had a baby, writing a book is reminiscent of this experience – hard, and worth it.

The first time you try to write a book, you find might yourself feeling overwhelmed, facing self-doubt, questioning your ability, or weighed down by fatigue. Those who follow through must decide to keep taking action in the face of fear and doubt. Day after day, they keep going. Even if you only spend 15 minutes a day on your book, you must keep showing up.

When I wrote my first book, I kept getting lost in the manuscript. *Did I already say this? I feel like I already wrote about this.* My days were filled with repeatedly pressing the Ctrl + F keys to look up words to see if I was repeating myself.

At one point, I realized that sitting down and simply writing wasn't a particularly organized or strategic approach. Instead, I thought about the key topics I wanted to write about, which became the chapters in the table of contents.

Once the content was outlined, I typed each chapter heading at the top of a page. These chapter headings provided containers I could jump around in to write where I felt inspired. For me, writing in order felt restrictive. I have to follow the inspiration, so I rarely write a book from start to finish in the order of the table of contents.

I also discovered if I stepped back too long from the manuscript, I started forgetting everything I had written up to that point. This caused time-consuming rereads of everything I had written so I could make forward progress.

I quickly discovered it was better to write even 10 minutes on days I didn't feel like writing, or didn't have time to write, to avoid the need to get back up to speed on the content over and over again.

Because producing a book is one heck of a commitment, you should choose to write about a subject you care deeply about, from your point of view and experience. You will question if your book is needed in the market. There are so many books about *[insert your book topic]*. Remember, there are zero books on the market from your lived experience on that topic.

Before you consider authoring a book, you have to know *why* you want to write it. Your why is what will keep you moving forward. If your goal is making money, you could end up discouraged. Authors who earn sizable revenue have usually published multiple books. Breaking even after paying an editor and cover designer is a realistic goal for your first book.

Many other excellent reasons exist for penning a book. It can open doors and elevate your career. Here are other great reasons to write a book:

- Create diverse, passive income strategies
- Offer copies to prospective clients
- Generate speaking opportunities
- Reach more people to help them
- Position yourself as an authority
- Help solidify your ideas
- Gain media attention
- Sell your services
- Boost credibility
- Generate leads

Consider your reasons for authoring a book and get clear on your motivation and end goal. Knowing the end goal helps you feel successful, regardless of sales figures.

Do you still want to write a book? If so, let's keep going! I'm going to assume you want to avoid common mistakes first time authors make. Here are three mistakes to avoid:

Editing as you write – A book is an iterative process. After you write it, you can edit it with a fresh perspective. Beta readers will give you feedback. Your editor will make suggestions. Get the words out. They can be changed and improved through the process. Just write, even if it stinks. Editing each sentence as you write it will ensure your book never sees the light of day. You can proofread the previous day's work before you begin writing again, as long as you aren't hampering your progress.

Not setting daily writing goals – If you don't set daily goals, you lose sight of your progress. Reaching small goals helps you stay motivated. Writing a book is a large goal: break it down into achievable daily goals.

Trying to do too much – Before writing my first children's book, *You've Got Gifts!*, I met with a consultant, Wendy Gilhula, author of the PIKA bunny series. After I explained my book, she said, "That's four books." Her advice was priceless. Cramming multiple books into one is a common mistake.

My first book took longer to write than any I've written since, regardless of word count. Lessons learned make every book easier. But writing a book never becomes easy.

My advice is to set a daily writing goal. An average nonfiction book is 50,000 words. Avoid books over 80,000 words—it's a sign of bloat. If your book is 80,000 words, it won't be after an editor gets a hold of it. For your first book, I don't recommend setting aggressive writing goals at the beginning. Focus on building a habit of consistency first. Once you have established consistency, you can increase your intensity.

To determine a daily goal, use a formula.

Total words ÷ days until due = daily goal (for writing daily)

Example: 50,000 ÷ 90 = 555.5 words per day

If you don't have a writing deadline, track your word count over the course of several days to determine what is reasonable for you to accomplish.

Finally, here are tips for building consistency, which is key with most success. Many points in the process will make you want to quit. I always feel each book I write seems terrible when I start writing it. Keep at it. Go back and read something you wrote that is an area of your expertise two weeks or more after writing it. You'll be surprised at how your perspective changes. You might even find yourself saying, "Hey, that sounds smart!"

Here are some tips to stay on track with writing:

1. Find the intersection where you are most passionate and where you can help, entertain, or inspire people. Avoid writing a book you don't have a strong pull to write. You'll procrastinate or quit.

2. Select a due date. I use Excel to create formulas to track when my book is due, today's date, and how many words I must write daily to meet the deadline. I open the spreadsheet daily to assess progress. My goal is usually 1,000 words daily, which I almost always exceed. I track how many words I write each session to see forward progress.

3. Schedule your writing and write even if you don't feel like it. Motivation follows action. By the time you get into the swing of writing, you'll be motivated and even meet or surpass your daily goal.

4. Build in commitment. Pick a friend or two as accountability partners to share how many words you've written. A quick text after each writing day is one idea. You could even join a writer's accountability group on social media.

5. Choose a time to write when you tend to be at your best. Are you a morning person or a night owl? Write accordingly.

6. Create an outline up front to guide your writing to make it easier. This can also reduce writer's block.

7. Capture your ideas as they occur. Keep a notepad and pen by your bed and use a voice recorder app. While writing this book, I had a flurry of ideas I captured on my phone during runs. You think you'll remember your bursts of inspiration but trust me, you won't. An electronic note app on your phone is also a great solution if you don't prefer the voice app.

8. Listen to podcasts or read interviews related to your subject matter. Give credit where it's due for quotes and concepts, and then expand on them and tell your own stories to back up the concepts. (People often search themselves online and appreciate when credit is given.) The conversations might also spark

new insights you can share in your book. Sharing a fresh perspective or a creative new application adds value to your readers.

We covered a lot of ground in this book. Our goal has been to help you navigate the ins and outs of running a successful coaching or consulting business and give you high quality tools to help you be an even better coach. Many who start a coaching business won't make it. We want you to be among the success stories.

To recap, we believe you should know why coaching businesses tend to fail. So, our last chapter shares the top ten reasons. You will be able to see just how well *Ready, Set, Coach!* has prepared you.

28

—————— ☙ ——————

WHY COACHING
BUSINESSES FAIL

Kristin

International Coaching Federation shared in their 2017 annual report that 82 percent of coaching businesses fail within the first two years. Why? Most coaches either go broke or burn out. We wrote *Ready, Set, Coach!* because we want to help you build a successful practice that you thrive working in. We have shared many lessons learned in our collective 40+ year coaching journey. We shared stories, guidance, best practices, tools, opportunities for reflection and hope you feel better prepared.

Let's review the top ten reasons coaching businesses fail and where we've discussed solutions to these concerns:

#1: NOT CONVERTING PROSPECTS TO CLIENTS

An International Coaching Federation (ICF) global coaching client study reported 99 percent of individuals and companies who hire a coach are "satisfied or very satisfied" and 96 percent say they would repeat the process.[15]

In addition, the International Society for Performance Improvement reports that coaching has a 221 percent return on investment (ROI).[16] Nevertheless, coaching is considered a luxury item that many people do not proactively include in their budget.

Coaching is a significant investment and a prospective client must sense you can help her feel comfortable making such an investment. After exposure to your online presence, or speaking to you, the prospect should feel encouraged that you understand her problem. We discussed this in "The Role of a Coach" section in "Chapter 1: Coach Stories" and "Chapter 2: You, The Coach." In addition, she trusts you can help her move forward. Otherwise, you will not induce her to sign up for your coaching. We shared a trust framework in "Chapter 19: Coaching Process & Best Practices."

Finally, confusing messaging and unclear client outcomes don't translate well in the real world. Using language such as "I will lead you to enlightened transformation" is unlikely to instill confidence or lead clients to enter your coaching program. We covered connecting to clients throughout the book, with greatest concentration in "Chapter 4: Your Ideal Clients" and "Chapter 9: Messaging and Marketing."

#2: NOT STANDING OUT / WEAK BRAND

Every year more coaches enter the market. ICF estimates there are 71,000 professional coaches worldwide and 23,000 based in North America. Between 2015 and 2019, the number of professional coaches worldwide increased by thirty-three percent globally and thirty-three percent in North America, based on ICF's 2020 Global Coaching Study Final Report.[17]

One reason coaches present a weak brand is often a changing focus. Continual pivots of your services and overall brand convey a lack of clarity, expertise, or confusion about who you are and who you serve. You are unlikely to gain client confidence if you are throwing different ideas at the wall to see what sticks. One month you're a LinkedIn Lead Generation coach, the next a business coach, and then a public speaking coach. It can be tempting to change gears if you aren't getting clients, but the services you're offering are not likely the problem.

Becoming a successful coach requires consistency, commitment, and perseverance. Self-discovery work helps you resist the temptation to reinvent yourself every time the wind changes direction. We helped you gain clarity about what you do best that others need most so you can stop second guessing yourself in "Chapter 2: You: The Coach," "Chapter 3: Coach or Consultant?," and "Chapter 4: Your Ideal Clients."

As more coaches enter the market, it's vital to clearly position yourself to attract the attention of your target clients. We shared how to identify your target clients in "Chapter 4: Your Ideal Clients" and how to stand out and build a strong brand in "Chapter 5: Build Your Brand."

#3: LACKING BUSINESS DEVELOPMENT SKILLS

A fair assumption is most coaches would rather work *in* their business (coaching people) than *on* their business. Skills related to working on the business include planning and forecasting, managing expenses, taxes, turning data into information and knowing what to do with the insights, lead generation and attracting clients.

"Chapter 7: Starting a Business" includes resources for creating a start-up, calculating your start-up costs, Q&A about side hustles, and more. "Chapter 8: Financial Considerations" addressed target revenue, managing expenses, taxes, and investing back in your business. We also covered getting clients in "Chapter 14: Attract Clients." Finally, "Chapter 22: Assess Success: Yours & The Client's" introduced you to a simple data-driven approach to evaluate success.

#4: LACKING CONFIDENCE

To succeed in coaching, you need confidence to face uncertainty and overcome your fears. When you have self-confidence, you believe in yourself. When you lack self-confidence, it can lead you to set a low bar for yourself, not establish or pursue ambitious goals, and reap mediocre outcomes. Confidence is needed to stretch yourself, push yourself to your limits, and even grow beyond them.

An interesting side benefit of self-awareness work is the growth in confidence which results. If you are plagued with wavering confidence or self-doubt, "Chapter 2: You, the Coach" and "Chapter 3: Coach or Consultant?" offer self-awareness guidance. The entire third section of the book, "Coach!," will build your coaching confidence with access to a treasure chest of processes, tools, and coaching questions you can build upon or use as-is in your practice.

#5: Lacking a System or Process

If you approach prospective clients by saying, "All the answers are inside you, and I will help you find them," that could come across as ambiguous or questionable. Instead, if you have a straightforward process, potential clients have a more substantial reason to feel confident about your expertise.

Clients will be more interested to work with you if you have a clear, yet flexible, framework or process to help them. We helped you think through and test the steps of your entire process from proposals to coaching with a variety of proven methods including "Chapter 11: Proposals," "Chapter 12: Services & Pricing," "Chapter 18: Discovery Calls," "Chapter 19: Coach Process & Best Practices," and "Chapter 20: Assessments & Tools."

#6: Wasting Time on Low-Value Activities

Are you tinkering with your LinkedIn profile for the 27th time? Do you continually react to mistakes in your process? Do you spend endless hours in networking meetings with everyone who requests one? Do you spend hours working on documents you might never reference? Do you edit and tinker with your website until you get everything perfect? "Chapter 24: Time Management" in "Part III: Coach!" helps you figure out how to better prioritize and focus your attention and efforts as well as how to manage your time to avoid squandering your most precious resource.

#7: FEARING FAILURE

Statista reports as many as 41.2 percent of U.S. entrepreneurs experience the fear of failure.[18] In the UK, the number is 48.3 percent. For Germans, fear of failure hovers around 31 percent. Fear of failure is understandable and normal. You took a significant risk to start your own business, walking away from a steady pay check, or pivoting from an earlier area of expertise. Learning to cope and overcome fear is within your control and will allow you to refocus your attention and influence a positive mindset shift.

Remember, you see your failures, flaws, and mistakes more than others do. Preparation and the ability to course correct and adapt can help you avoid missteps that lead to failure. This entire book was written to spare you the mistakes we learned the hard way. We hope we have provided quality guidance to help eliminate or reduce fear of failure you might experience.

#8: Not Grasping The Value Of Your Services

When we don't accurately understand the value of our services, we price ourselves out of the market with unrealistically high rates if we *overestimate* our value. We must focus on the needs of the client over our own interests. Value is decided by the buyer not by our pricing.

Alternatively, if we low ball our prices and work our rear ends off for little profit, we *underestimate* our value and burn ourselves out in the process. We addressed how to approach pricing your services in "Chapter 12: Services & Pricing" and "Chapter 21: Group Coaching."

#9: Not Investing Wisely In The Business

Investing too much, too soon often breaks a business. So can waiting too long to invest in important areas. Employing a do-it-yourself approach on low value tasks, refusing to hire a part-time assistant, and shying away from investing in experts who can ramp up your business faster are some ways small business owners do not invest wisely in their business. We reviewed expenses that can likely wait, and those you should consider prioritizing, in "Chapter 8: Financial Considerations" and "Chapter 16: Hire the Right Assistant."

#10: Relying On Passive Marketing

Passive marketing refers to sitting back and waiting for people to come to you. Once established, you *will* have clients coming to you and passive marketing should be part of your overall marketing strategy. As you build your business, sitting back and waiting for people to find you will not create action in your DMs, texts, and inbox.

In "Chapter 9: Messaging & Marketing" and "Chapter 14: Attract Clients," we provided stories and examples to help you actively market and win clients using both direct and soft selling strategies. And remember to make sure you are pursuing the right clients. "Chapter 4: Your Ideal Clients" covered this topic.

Beyond the ten reasons clients fail, *Ready, Set, Coach!* includes an abundance of other guidance to help you build a thriving coaching practice…Fast! Refer to this book – which one early reader dubbed "The Coach's Bible" – when you feel stuck, uncertain, or need inspiration.

FINAL THOUGHTS

———————— C3 ————————

"The prizes of life we fail to win,
when we doubt our power within."
- Unknown

Boldly pursuing one's goals and dreams is not for the faint of heart. Some days you will feel unstoppable on the mountaintop, while others you will feel overwhelmed in the valley.

"What was I thinking?" your mind will say. Cling to why you became a coach when your inner voice tries to steal your confidence and replace it with doubt. *Your "why" must be stronger than your worries.*

Remember, you are your own greatest asset.

And nothing that's worth anything is ever easy.

POSTSCRIPT

───────── ℭℬ ─────────

My Mom Used to Say
A Year's Wisdom for A Lifetime of Success
Written by Judith C. Spear
In memory of Rhoda Ann Rhodes

This too shall pass.

Haste makes waste.

Water seeks its own level.

Be careful what you wish for.

If you don't ask, you don't get.

Nothing ventured, nothing gained.

You can't fix what you don't know.

Necessity is the mother of invention.

A problem named is a problem half solved.

You bid the devil good day when you meet him.

A coward dies a thousand deaths, a hero dies but one.

A journey of a thousand miles begins with the first step.

As long as it isn't illegal or immoral, there's a time and a place for everything.

There are very few missed opportunities, there are plenty of delayed opportunities.

Rhoda Ann Rhodes was a remarkable woman. We lost her suddenly March 25, 1991, one month after her eightieth birthday. Not a day goes by that I don't think of her. Wise beyond belief, her teachings have become even more useful as I married, had my own children and built a successful management consulting practice. On more occasions than I can count, my mother reached out in wisdom to others with just the right insight.

Rhoda Ann Rhodes was born February 25, 1911, on the Mohawk reserve at Ohsweken in Southern Ontario, Canada. One of six, her childhood was fraught with difficulty, and she married at seventeen hoping to find peace and stability. Instead, she found nine children and the challenge of raising most of them through the difficulties of the Great Depression and World War II.

As I was growing up in the 1950s and '60s, she would often talk to me about her observations of life as she cooked or ironed. These pearls of wisdom were sprinkled through fascinating stories about her early life in a world a million miles from the safe and happy place she had created for me and my two younger brothers, a second family that accidentally happened with a spread of seven years between me and the youngest of the first six children born to her and my father, William Andrew Johns.

My mother did three things that I believe gave me a solid start in life. First and foremost, I always knew that I was very important to her. She was not a person who regularly told us she loved us or hugged us spontaneously, but you knew that every moment of her day was spent thinking about how she would provide for us, no matter what.

The challenge of feeding her own first six children plus her brother's two daughters during the depression haunted her. My father was always self-employed and, by his own admission, was never good with money. But whatever he made, he would bring home to mother, and her job was to stretch those dollars. While no longer desperately poor by the time I was born, she still had to be careful.

The second thing came from two stories she told that I will never forget. The first story was about her awkwardness as a chubby preteen. She loved to read and escaped the challenges of life through books, squirreling away feeding her body and her mind. At thirteen, she discovered dancing. She loved it so much she would find ways to dance daily, all by herself, wherever she could. The weight fell off as her skill skyrocketed. She thought of nothing else. In 1926, a miracle happened.

The New York City Rockettes held an open audition in Buffalo, just down the road from her home in Niagara Falls, New York. Without her mother's knowledge, she maneuvered herself into the audition and was accepted from among hundreds of other hopefuls. But her mother refused to let a 15-year-old go to New York City, and her dream was smashed.

Her other story was about how she loved school and craved an education. She knew instinctively it was her ticket to a better life. At sixteen, she was forced to leave school in her senior year to get a job. These were the two biggest disappointments of her life and decades later she would cry whenever she relived those experiences.

Her mission became showing possibilities to her children, hoping they would not live the heart-wrenching disappointments of her early years. And that was the second thing she developed in me: look for the possibilities. No matter what, find options.

The third gift she gave me was the belief I could have, be, or do anything I was willing to work for. She was resourceful and wanted us to have the same skill.

"Women's Lib" came to my mother in a powerful way. It was as if she suddenly realized her life was far from over, and she had the power to change it. So, thirty years after the heartbreak of leaving school, she returned to learn basic accounting.

My mother never learned to drive, so the next obvious challenge was getting a driver's license. My father was less than encouraging and said he doubted she'd pass! Like a red flag to a bull, he inspired her to prove him wrong. She signed up for lessons and, years later, credited her driving instructor as her "savior."

With license in hand, she was ready for anything. Because she felt homemaking was her only real skill, she found a housekeeper job with a well-off family. As her courage grew, and much to the regret of the family she helped, she decided to try working in a kitchen and landed in an elegant restaurant, complete with maître d'. I am sure the restaurant manager, a local legend, saw my mother's potential in spite of her humble background and experience.

In short order, she was managing the kitchen and reveling in her expanding career. Public transit carried her to her housekeeping and restaurant jobs. But when she earned her accounting certificate, she must have decided that it was time for a "business" job. She was always drawn to health care and applied for a job assisting the executive director of a hospital. Again, someone saw her potential and she was in.

Her small hoard scrimped together over several years supplied the down payment on her first car. At the age of fifty-six, she had a "real" job and a chance to make her mark. Her life, a life she could direct, was finally in her hands. She had arrived. And she was in the driver's seat.

ACKNOWLEDGEMENTS

———— ✂ ————

Kristin:

I'm thankful to my grandmother, Rhoda Ann Rhodes. The "A" in Kristin A. Sherry comes from her, and it is with love that the book is dedicated to her memory. I had her in my life for nineteen short years. Without her, I wouldn't have my extraordinary mother Judi Spear who, through the best example, taught me how to coach, to love, give, and pursue my dreams.

Thanks to God for putting these women in my life.

To the beta readers who gave their time to take this book from good to great: Kimberly Tilley, Paul Crothall, Carrie Stiles, and Loreen (the new) Marshall (in town).

To the YouMap® coaches and clients who asked me to coach them, giving me the rich experiences I can share to help others.

To my incredible husband Xander. You go above and beyond to support me and YouMap LLC. It's sweet you never accept copies of my books and insist on buying them.

To the wonderful coaches who said yes when asked to be interviewed for this book. Kerri Twigg, Natasha Knight,

Victoria Volk, Amoreena Murray, and Diane Roesch. We are grateful.

Thank you to my publisher, *Black Rose Writing*. I appreciate your patience with this one.

Finally, to dad. I love you and I'm so glad you were here for this.

Judi:

Thank you to Kristin. Without her prodding and incredible book writing expertise, this book would never have become a reality.

To our coaching friends and colleagues who came out of the woodwork to be a part of the project.

To the six tremendous people who coached me over the years starting with my mother, Rhoda Ann Rhodes. The others are Victor J. Davis, Paul Mitchell, Jim Walter, Wilfred J. Larson and my husband, Wayne W. Spear. He believed in me long before I believed in myself.

To all the wonderful people who have allowed me to be their coach and enriched my life in the process.

ABOUT THE AUTHORS

Kristin A. Sherry is a bestselling, award-winning author, globally recognized career expert, and creator of the YouMap® profile (*2020 Career Innovator Award*). She is the managing partner of YouMap LLC, which certifies coaches, consultants and leaders in YouMap®. In addition to books for adults, Kristin authors books to build confidence and self-awareness in children.

Judi Spear, Founder of RV Rhodes, Inc., her US-based company and Spear-Rhodes, Ltd., her Canadian-based company, is an executive coach and facilitator who has coached over 50,000 people. She earned her bachelor's in business and master's in  Organizational Leadership and Communication. She is a certified management consultant and a designated board-certified coach and executive coach by the Center for Credentialing and Education (CCE).

CONNECT WITH THE AUTHORS

KRISTIN SHERRY

LinkedIn: linkedin.com/in/kristinsherry

Company Website: www.myyoumap.com

Author website: kristinsherry.info

YouTube: youtube.com/c/kristinsherry

JUDI SPEAR

LinkedIn: linkedin.com/in/judispear

Website: rvrhodesinc.com

BOOKS BY KRISTIN A. SHERRY

If you enjoyed *Ready, Set, Coach!* we would appreciate if you would leave an online review. Thank you! We hope you enjoy Kristin A. Sherry's other books for adults and children published by *Black Rose Writing* and available where online books are sold or at blackrosewriting.com.

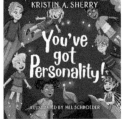

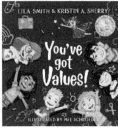
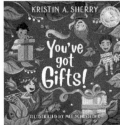

REFERENCES

1. Stoll G., Rieger, S., Lüdtke, O., Nagengast, B., Trautwein, U., Roberts, B.W., "Vocational interests assessed at the end of high school predict life outcomes assessed 10 years later over and above IQ and Big Five personality traits," *Journal of Personality and Sociology*, 2017 Jul; 113(1):167-184.

2. https://www.sba.gov/business-guide/10-steps-start-your-business. Retrieved March 3, 2022

3. https://www.sba.gov/business-guide/plan-your-business/calculate-your-startup-costs. Retrieved March 3, 2022.

4. https://www.sba.gov/business-guide/plan-your-business/write-your-business-plan. Retrieved March 3, 2022.

5. https://www.forbes.com/sites/allbusiness/2015/05/11/surviving-first-year-as-small-business-owner. Retrieved February 5, 2022.

6. https://smallbusiness.chron.com/average-time-reach-profitability-start-up-company-2318.html. Retrieved February 5, 2022.

7. Dreze, X., Hoch, S. J., & Purk, M. E. (1995). Shelf management and space elasticity. Journal of Retailing.

8. https://smallbiztrends.com/2016/10/customer-retention-statistics.html

9. Ibid.

10. Ibid.

11. Ibid.

12. Murphy, M., *"Why New Hires Fail (Emotional Intelligence vs. Skills),"* Leadership IQ, Retrieved September 28, 2019 from
https://www.leadershipiq.com/blogs/leadershipiq/35354 241-why-new-hires-fail-emotional-intelligence-vs-skills.

13. Adapted from Enlightened Leadership: Getting to the heart of change, by Ed Oakley & Doug Krug,
Simon & Schuster (1991).

14. https://www.valamis.com/hub/adult-learning-principles. Retrieved March 15, 2022

15. https://coachfederation.org/research/global-coaching-study

16. Ibid.

17. Ibid.

18. https://www.statista.com/statistics/268788/fear-of-failure-start-ups-in-leading-economic-nations/

APPENDIX

—————— Ⳝ ——————

Ready, Set, Coach! supporting videos found at bit.ly/rscvideos

Download the Coach Canvas template at myyoumap.com/ready-set-coach.

Chapter 1: Coach Stories

The Role of a Coach:

#1: To encourage a person about his or her situation
#2: To move that person to action

The 3 C's of Coaching:

#1: Coach what you know
#2: Combine what you know with your abilities
#3: Care deeply about the work

Chapter 2: You, the Coach

Sample Coach Canvas

(blank template on next page)

Strengths	**Top Values**	**Top 5 Skills**	**Traits**
Maximizer	Love/Connection	Innovate	Encouraging
Futuristic	Faith	Strategize	Enthusiastic
Strategic	Autonomy	Write	Insightful
Ideation	Making a	Ideate	Resourceful
Input	Difference	Instruct/Train	Strategic
	Fun		Curious
	Balance	**Interests**	Imaginative
	Creativity	Thinker	Creative
	Meaningful Work	Persuader	
	Wisdom		
	Achievement		

How I Encourage Clients
I recognize and pinpoint greatness in people and help them see it, clearly and convincingly.

How I Move Them to Action
I generate strategic ideas clients have not considered, along with practical steps to take.

My Background/Experience
Industries: Healthcare, Education, Training, Coaching

Roles:
Operations Management
L & D Leadership

My Unique Contribution
Strategic and visionary leader who maximizes others to achieve greater success through the creation of innovative programs.

Ideal Client Traits
Self-motivated
Avoids excuses
Achievement-oriented
Service-oriented

Who I Help
Coaches, Leaders, Consultants, Career Counselors, HR Professionals

Coach Canvas

Strengths	Top Values	Top 5 Skills	Traits
		Interests	

How I Encourage Clients	How I Move Them to Action

My Background/Experience	My Unique Contribution

Ideal Client Traits	Who I Help

Adapted from the Lean Canvas by Ash Maurya

The Four Pillars of Career Fit™

THE FOUR PILLARS OF CAREER FIT™

HOW YOU WORK (STRENGTHS) | WHY YOU WORK (VALUES)

WHO YOU ARE (PERSONALITY) | WHAT YOU ENJOY DOING (SKILLS)

Find My Top 5 CliftonStrengths

store.gallup.com/p/en-us/10108/top-5-cliftonstrengths

Summary of the 34 CliftonStrengths

Strengths on the left are "people (outward) facing." Strengths on the right are "inward-facing." For definitions: gallup.com/cliftonstrengths/en/253715/34-cliftonstrengths-themes.aspx

Summary of the 34 CliftonStrengths (cont.)

People-facing Strengths		Inward-facing Strengths	
Relationship-building	*Influencing*	*Executing*	*Thinking*
Adaptability	Activator	Achiever	Analytical
Connectedness	Command	Arranger	Context
Developer	Communication	Belief	Futuristic
Empathy	Competition	Consistency	Ideation
Harmony	Maximizer	Deliberative	Input
Includer	Self-Assurance	Discipline	Intellection
Individualization	Significance	Focus	Learner
Positivity	WOO	Responsibility	Strategic
Relator		Restorative	

My Skills

YouMap® Preferred Skills Inventory

Directions to complete the skills inventory are below the table.

YOUMAP® PREFERRED SKILLS INVENTORY

Administration
- Budget
- Categorize
- Organize
- Paperwork

Conceptual/Creative
- Abstract Thinking
- Ambiguity, Deal w/
- Create Images
- Design
- Envision
- Ideate
- Improvise
- Innovate
- Strategize

Interpersonal
- Advise
- Collaborate
- Instruct/Train
- Liaise
- Manage Emotions
- Mediate
- Use Intuition

Leadership
- Initiate Change
- Lead Others
- Mentor
- Motivate

Manage Process/Projects
- Customer Service
- Execute
- Expedite
- Handle Change
- Manage Logistics
- Manage Time
- Monitor
- Multi-Task
- Plan

Research/Analysis
- Analyze
- Assess
- Interview for Information
- Observe
- Research
- Study

Sales
- Competitiveness
- Negotiate
- Present/Perform
- Risk-Taking
- Sell

Supervise
- Decision Making
- Delegate
- Hiring/Staffing
- Manage Others

Technical/Mechanical
- Computer Skills
- Edit
- Estimate
- Mechanical
- Numeric Accuracy
- Test
- Write

Following are 55 common skills.

Read each skill definition. Imagine using the skill regularly. If you are **good at a skill *and* enjoy using it regularly**, or think you might, place a check (✔) beside it. These are your *preferred* skills. Highlight your preferred skills in the previous table to confirm your preferred skill categories (leadership, interpersonal, etc.).

- ☐ *Abstract Thinking* – Form and develop ideas and concepts
- ☐ *Advise* – Provide counsel, guidance, direction, information or enlightenment to others
- ☐ *Ambiguity, Deal with* – Act when details are unclear; comfortable leaving issues open; at ease with the unknown
- ☐ *Analyze* – Examine methodically and in detail, typically for purposes of explanation and interpretation
- ☐ *Assess* – Evaluate, assess or judge to determine quality or capability
- ☐ *Budget* – Estimate costs, revenue, and resources over a specified period
- ☐ *Categorize* – Arrange people or things into classifications according to shared qualities or characteristics
- ☐ *Change, Handle* – Embrace or deal well with change to work priorities or focus
- ☐ *Collaborate* – Willingly follow or lead, show trust and support of co-workers; build partnerships
- ☐ *Competitiveness* – Enjoy challenging goals, being measured against those goals; strong desire to win
- ☐ *Computer Skills* – Use computers and related technology, such as Microsoft Office, efficiently, with a range of skills
- ☐ *Create Images* – Illustrate through drawing, sketches, photography or other visual means

- *Customer Service* – Assist, advise and solve customer problems and support customers appropriately
- *Decision Making* – Frequently decide outcomes of options and determine which choice is the best for a situation
- *Delegate* – Assign tasks to others; explain why a task is important and the expected results
- *Design* – Plan the look and function or workings of a program, product, or object before it is created or made
- *Edit* – Read or revise written or printed materials
- *Envision* – Picture or envision what's possible
- *Estimate* – Roughly calculate or determine the value, number, quantity, or extent of
- *Execute* – Implement and follow through on policies, plans, or programs
- *Expedite* – Restructure actions or solve problems to accomplish tasks quicker
- *Hiring/Staffing* – Use good judgment about people; make selection decisions that result in good performers
- *Ideate* – Generate or think up ideas
- *Improvise* – Perform or think on one's feet, that is, without planning or preparing
- *Initiate Change* – Introduce or influence new ways of doing things
- *Innovate* – Welcome, encourage and seek continual improvement on a small or large scale
- *Instruct/Train* – Show or explain to someone how to do something
- *Interview for Information* – Ask questions using insight to obtain information
- *Lead Others* – Enjoy taking responsibility and directing others; take charge of introducing necessary change

- *Liaise* – Communicate or cooperate between people or organizations to facilitates close working relationships
- *Manage Logistics* – Manage events; handle detailed coordination of people, facilities, or supplies
- *Manage Emotions*– Display ability to realize, readily accept, and deal with the feelings of others
- *Manage Others* – Directly manage others and provide performance feedback
- *Manage Time* – Use one's time wisely and productively to meet deadlines
- *Mechanical* – Repair, fix or operate machinery
- *Mediate* – Intervene between people in a dispute to reach agreement
- *Mentor* – Guide, coach, or counsel less experienced employees or students
- *Monitor* – Track people, activities, information to confirm fairness or correctness
- *Motivate* – Bring out the best in people; keep others enthusiastic and involved
- *Multi-task* – Deal with more than one task or project at the same time
- *Negotiate* – Attempt to reach an agreement or compromise with others
- *Numeric accuracy* – Solve numerical problems, work with numbers or look for patterns in numbers
- *Observe* – Notice, see, perceive, discern and identify something observed as significant
- *Organize* – Keep work area neat, follow an orderly approach and keep things organized
- *Paperwork* – Comfortable with repetition and attention to detail and maintaining accurate and timely records

- *Plan* – Specify steps for a project before beginning and prepare for potential problems before they occur
- *Present/Perform* – Speak or perform in front of an audience
- *Research* – Engage in data discovery such as conducting online research
- *Risk-Taking* – Willing to leave one's comfort zone; focus on reward over potential for failure
- *Sell* – Persuade and promote; optimistic and does not take no for an answer
- *Strategize* – Identify long-term goals; work backwards to identify the most effective option of the alternatives
- *Study* – Read written information in a thorough or careful way
- *Test* – Examine critically to determine accuracy, precision or quality
- *Use Intuition* – Understand something immediately using insight without need for conscious reasoning
- *Write* – Make an effort to put thoughts in writing, be concise, descriptive and keep readers in mind

My Personality-Based Interests

The Six Holland Interest Types

Doer:

Prefers work that involves practical, hands-on solutions to problems. Values things they can see, touch, and use. Likes to work with their hands, often works outside with machinery, tools, or animals

Thinker:

Intellectual, curious, and reserved. Likes to solve problems and engage in challenges. Will often choose work that involves ideas and heavy mental lifting.

Creator:

Imaginative, creative, original, independent, and expressive. Inspired to create through activities such as music, writing, drawing, dance, photography, or art.

Helper:

Interested in serving society and making a difference. Likes to help people, and their work is most often centered around others. They are helpful, friendly, loyal, generous, and trustworthy. They gravitate toward nonprofit, education, healthcare, and social work.

Persuader:

Often deals with business, leadership, or politics. Involved in making decisions, starting up and carrying out projects. Likes selling ideas or things. Generally energetic, ambitious, dominant, outgoing, and competitive.

Organizer:

Provides the structure, process, and order that organizations need to run effectively. Generally methodical, detail-oriented, cautious, organized, responsible, and quality-oriented. They are the glue that holds an organization together.

Unique Contribution Statement Video Tutorial
bit.ly/UCStatementTutorial
(URL is case-sensitive)

Chapter 5: Your Ideal Clients

How to Use Credibility Stories by Kerri Twigg

www.linkedin.com/pulse/how-use-credibility-stories-career-growth-kerri-twigg/

Chapter 7: Starting a Business

Chicken & Pig Business Model

STAR'S BUSINESS MODELS

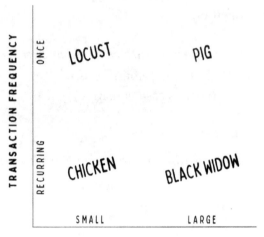

SBA 10 Steps to Start Your Business

https://www.sba.gov/business-guide/10-steps-start-your-business

SBA Calculate Your Startup Costs

https://www.sba.gov/business-guide/plan-your-business/calculate-your-startup-costs

SBA Business Plan Guide

sba.gov/business-guide/plan-your-business/write-your-business-plan

NerdWallet Business Startup Costs

nerdwallet.com/article/small-business/how-to-calculate-startup-costs-for-small-business

Chapter 24: Time Management

Impact/Effort Grid

		Low	Medium	High
IMPACT	*High*	1		2
	Medium		3	
	Low	4		5
		Low	Medium	High
			EFFORT	

SECTION	ACTION STEPS
1: High Impact/Low Effort	*Quick Hits!* Start here. These are easy tasks to help surpass your goal.
2: High Impact/High Effort	*Plan for the Future* These are major tasks that take a lot of effort with big payoff. These might require more planning or people.
3: Medium Impact/ Medium Effort	*Options, Options, Options* These activities offer promise, but require work. Spread these out over time or delegate them.

4: Low Impact/Low Effort	*Low Hanging Fruit* You might feel Low Impact activities should be ignored. Sometimes they're needed for a quick win. Consider them carefully but stay focused on High Impact activities.
5: Low Impact/High Effort	*Why Bother?* Think twice before doing tasks that rob resources with low payoff. Perhaps someone important asked you to undertake these tasks. Show her the high payoff/low effort tasks you've identified.
Other Squares	*Use Your Judgment* Decide for each task. In general, High Impact tasks are the best place to begin.

Chapter 25: Passive Income & Intellectual Property

TESS Trademark Search
https://www.uspto.gov/trademarks/search

Chapter 28: Why Coaching Businesses Fail

10 Reasons Coaching Businesses Fail

1. Not converting prospects to clients
2. Not standing out / weak brand
3. Lacking business development skills
4. Lacking confidence
5. Lacking a coaching system or process
6. Wasting time on low-value activities

7. Fearing failure
8. Not grasping the value of your services
9. Not investing wisely in the business
10. Relying on passive marketing

We hope you enjoyed reading this title from:

www.blackrosewriting.com

Subscribe to our mailing list – *The Rosevine* – and receive **FREE**
books, daily deals, and stay current with news
about upcoming releases and our hottest authors.
Scan the QR code below to sign up.

Already a subscriber? Please accept a sincere thank you for
being a fan of Black Rose Writing authors.

View other Black Rose Writing titles at
www.blackrosewriting.com/books and use promo code
PRINT to receive a **20% discount** when purchasing.

CPSIA information can be obtained
at www.ICGtesting.com
Printed in the USA
BVHW082200130922
646893BV00009B/481